the
psychological
manager

change:
increasing resilience through transition

acknowledgements

I'd like to thank pretty much the same people that I thanked last time, because they continue to be important in my life and continue to be fabulous. You know who you are.

I'd also like to say a more specific thank you to Amanda who has beautifully edited and formatted this book, just like she did the first time. Any remaining errors are purely mine.

the
psychological
manager

change:
increasing resilience through transition

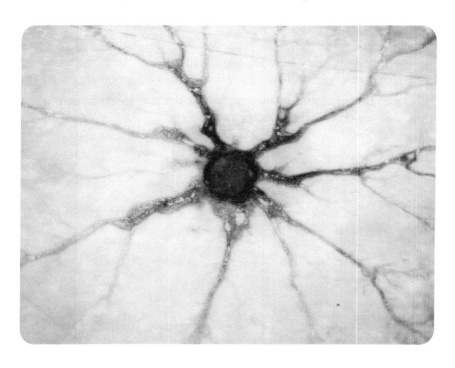

peter storr

about the author

Peter Storr is a Chartered Psychologist with 30 years of organisational experience. He has led both large and small teams in the private and public sectors and has many years' experience as a management coach. Peter has worked as both an external management consultant and an internal Occupational Psychology consultant at the BBC. Most recently he was strategic Head of Organisation Development at a London-based Russell Group university.

His expertise is centred on management and leadership: helping managers to lead and manage individuals and teams, designing and running managerial assessment and development centres, coaching and coaching training, group facilitation and designing management development programmes. He is married, lives in Berkshire and still hasn't grown any chickens.

This is Peter's third book after (CMI-nominated Management Book of the Year) *The Psychological Manager: Improve Your Performance Conversations* (available at **www.thepsychologicalmanager.com**) and *Get That Job in 7 Simple Steps*, published by Collins.

Peter runs his own consultancy, dealing with all aspects of management and team development, assessment and management development project work.

He can be contacted at **thepsychologicalmanager@gmail.com**. Let him know what you think of this book, or just say hello.

contents

foreword

by Zofia Ashmore

Learning and Talent Development Manager
University of Greenwich

In my first week of joining a new organisation, I attended a general staff meeting on the development of a new strategy. The Chief Executive's (CEO) presentation was lucid in its articulation of the drivers for change and in identifying ways in which the institution needed to adapt. During the question-and-answer session I started experiencing a growing sense of confusion, uncertainty and frustration. I was surprised by staff reactions, and I felt that the majority of people 'just didn't get it' and that they were 'stuck in their ways'. After all, it was evident that the organisation had to make changes to the way it conducted its activities – there were already precedents in the sector – and the CEO's arguments seemed logical.

At the time, I didn't fully appreciate that while articulating the urgency of the need to adapt to different ways of working in order to meet external challenges, the CEO was also introducing a high degree of uncertainty among staff regarding the potential impact of the proposed changes on fundamental structures, individuals and roles. My sense of being taken by surprise by the questions and reactions of those around me is indicative of the differing perceptions, and therefore meanings, that were being formed during the session. Where

I saw opportunity, others sensed threat; the CEO's proposals were being questioned, the rationale for change being met with reasons why there was no need to alter anything. These differing views on the purpose of the organisation, how it should function and how it should adapt to challenges illustrate a set of fundamental variations in experiences and assumptions that may be explained by the concept of 'organisation-in-the-mind': a set of 'mental pictures' that an individual holds as an 'amalgam of ideas and experiences which are unique to him and which form and shape themselves in a particular pattern', and which impact on how individuals relate and communicate in the workplace.[1] Every one of us in the room had our own mental image of the organisational reality inside of us, and we each made the assumption that everyone else's image was identical to ours, while in fact they were quite different.

I find this a useful paradigm through which to explore the concept of change in its organisational context and its impact on individuals. After all, change is all around us and it continuously affects what we do and how we are at work. The political and economic drivers create a volatile world full of complexity and ambiguity. Rapid technological advances, combined with demographic societal shifts, generate pressure mixed with uncertainty. Whether we are the 'architects' of a change initiative, or a 'change agent' developing an implementation plan, or an individual just minding our own business and hoping to make it to retirement without too much disruption – none of us are immune to change.

Change affects us in our personal spaces too: relationships, job changes, life events, educational challenges, lifestyle choices – they all continue to occur and demand a response. Due to the nature and pace of these multiple and often overlapping changes that we encounter day to day, what's increasingly required of every one of us is that we get on with it, deal with uncertainty, overcome fear and resistance, manage our own and others' emotions, engage with the process, and emerge from it at the other end – relatively unscathed, and able to deal with yet another set of fluctuating circumstances with which life has decided to present us, or that we have chosen to carry out ourselves. In other words, there is an increasing need for us to be resilient when facing change, and to look after our own wellbeing in order to meet its demands.

There are many models of organisational change in management literature, and they're all in their own ways useful when it comes to analysing the different phases or steps of the process in order to come up with the most effective way

1   Hutton, J., Bazalgette, J. & Reed, B. (1997). 'Organisation-in-the-mind' in Neumann, J., Kellner, K. & Dawson-Shepherd, A. (eds) *Developing Organisational Consultancy*. London: Routledge, p 115.

of designing and implementing it. What seems to have been sparsely discussed in mainstream literature until recently is the human dimension of organisational change: the messy emotions that tend to erupt and get in the way of a logical process and rational debate about the pros and cons of a particular change initiative.

As the world continues to evolve and many traditional organisations have all but 'vanished' by becoming more fragmented, virtual and networked,[2] there is a growing sense that the negative and disruptive aspects of change can be all the more overpowering because the traditional support structures are no longer available. This places additional demands on those of us who are leaders and managers in the modern organisational context: we have to find fresh ways of understanding change as well as its impact, and consequently develop innovative, holistic approaches to how we deal with change and support others in dealing with it themselves. Peter Storr's book helps us do exactly that.

Through his evolutionary perspective on change and the exploration of the mechanisms that underpin our unconscious reactions to it, Peter helps us orientate ourselves in the complexities and mysteries of why we behave the way we do, and he draws out practical insights, focusing on what we can learn from it. His unique ability to convey complex, scientific concepts from neuroscience and psychology in easy-to-understand language, using examples from everyday life, and making it fun as we go along, serves to de-mystify the concept of change and prepares us for the exciting journey of taking charge. Peter also provides a range of helpful worksheets and checklists, which will ensure that our learning is ongoing, applicable in a variety of contexts, and that we can adapt it to suit the specific needs of our organisations and teams as well as our own.

I've known and worked with Peter for a number of years, and I've watched with great interest his own journey of change: as a manager and strategic leader, a trainer, a coach, a consultant, a writer and above all, as a genuine, warm and supportive human being. He is infectiously positive and curious about people, with a depth of knowledge and a real passion for creating innovative ways of connecting it all and illuminating it for us so that we can take something away and make it work, just as we need it. This book will inform as well as support any manager who wants to dip into it to learn more about a particular topic, or explore a broader theme, or just skip straight to the appendices for a quick-fix solution. It is invaluable in navigating the many aspects of change in the modern world of work.

---

2   Cooper, A. & Dartington, T. (2004). 'The vanishing organisation: organisational containment in a networked world' in Huffington, C., Armstrong, D., Halton, W., Hoyle, L. & Pooley, J. (eds) *Working Below the Surface. The Emotional Life of Contemporary Organisations*. London: Karnac, pp 127–150.

introduction

One of the things I love about my chosen profession of Psychology is that it applies to pretty much every aspect of our lives. But when writing a book about it, this can be a problem – not so much what to write about, but what to leave out. As a general rule of thumb, I prefer to write about stuff I know something about, so the form and content of my books – and this is now my third – follow pretty much the subject areas of my practice.

Over the last couple of years an increasing amount of my work, as a facilitator as well as a coach, is in the areas of change and resilience. The two are intricately linked, and most books treat them as separate things. In my first book[1] I attempted to condense all the content that's usually taught on management development programmes into one place, because people are busy living lives and actually doing stuff. This is also what I've tried to do here, based on another set of courses that I run. Change, resilience, influence, self-development, thinking biases – they're all inextricably linked with each other

---

1   *The Psychological Manager: Improve Your Performance Conversations* (2012).

and make, if we squint in just the right way, what my good friend (who'll remain nameless[2]) would no doubt call a 'journey'.

I had a lot of compliments (thanks, Mum) about my first book and its informal style, so I've gone down the same route this time. We learn best when we enjoy ourselves, so I wanted to write something that I'd enjoy reading myself and that would occasionally make me smile, despite the seriousness at times of the subject matter. The point is, all of us have to deal with change constantly and it can wear us down if we're not careful. In my view we need all the help we can get – and this is my primary driver in writing this book.

Our brain is the most complex thing in the known universe, and it's still a bit rubbish. It gets confused. It makes us behave in ways we don't want, it makes us think about things in unhelpful ways, and don't get me started on feelings. It can seem at times like it (i.e. life) is all happening *to* us, instead of controlled *by* us.

I think there's something we can do about this. The first step to taking control is, of course, knowledge and awareness, so reading this book is a good first step towards increasing your resilience through life's challenges. In addition, the worksheets (in the Appendices) will add some structure to your thinking by taking you through reflection exercises. These are also available to download from my website (**www.thepsychologicalmanager.com**) because some people work that way.

As in my other two books, I've drawn on four main sources:

- An up-to-date knowledge of psychological theory from my own studies as an Occupational Psychologist, subsequent reading and continuing professional development.
- My work as a trainer, facilitator and coach.
- My own 30 years' worth of experience in and around organisations.
- Life.

finding your way around

section 1 👤 the context of change

Everything is changing all the time, so having to deal with it is inevitable. This section looks at the drivers of change and how we can influence it – or even create it.

---

2   Jane.

section 2 👥 how (and why) we react to change

We're wired, pretty much, to dislike change. Which, bearing in mind Section 1, doesn't really help, does it? This section looks at why this is, the implications of the way our brains are structured and the typical impact of change, along with what causes any individual differences in how we deal with it.

section 3 👥 change and you: self-awareness

In this section we use the underpinning theory and model of emotional intelligence to help us explore how we can become more self-aware, and how this can help us become more resilient during change.

section 4 👥 increase your resilience

Section 4 is where we begin to take control. It looks at how to master our thoughts, feelings and behaviours, and challenge the unhelpful beliefs we may have that get in the way. It then moves on to providing support in developing new, more positive habits, and looks at ways that we can look after ourselves better through this process.

section 5 👥 take your team through change

This section turns our attention to the extra things we can do to positively lead a team or department through a change process to limit and deal with any resistance we might run into – from our team or our stakeholders.

This book is for anyone who wants to deal as constructively and positively as possible through changes imposed on them or that they'd like to impose themselves. I reckon that means pretty much all of us. I hope you find it interesting, useful and even a tad entertaining.

Peter Storr
C.Psychol
March 2017

the context of change

'Survival is the ability to swim in strange waters'

Frank Herbert, *Dune*

the only constant

I'll be honest with you here. If I hear that hoary old chestnut 'Change is the only constant' one more time, I'll saw off my own leg with a rusty spanner. It's so painfully obvious and overused that it fails to have any meaning. It's also untrue.[1] But, of course, like many trite and annoying sayings – and those pithy phrases posted on your LinkedIn timeline every day – it's sort of true. The world is constantly changing. Society is. The world of work is. And we are.

Who we are changes. Who we were changes (or at least our perception of who we were). Who we want to be changes. What we want to achieve changes. The circumstances of our lives both at home and at work change. Constantly.

Curses. Perhaps that annoying saying has a point after all.

---

1   Pedants among you will think about Pi, or, of course, Euler's constant: approximately equal to 2.71828, and is the limit of $(1 + 1/n)^n$ as n approaches infinity, an expression that arises in the study of compound interest. I looked it up. It's probably not what they meant, though.

dealing with change

We'd better get used to change, then. But it's hard. And most of us don't like it. Some do, and actively search for it, but most of us don't – or at the very least, it makes us uncomfortable. Dealing with uncertainty and ambiguity is a life skill that most of us would rather not develop. And it appears, if the Leadership literature is anything to go by, that it's becoming increasingly important in this new technological age, where Moore's Law (computing power doubles every two years or so) still applies 40 years after it was posited. It changes everything. I use no more than 20% of my phone's capabilities (and that's pushing it) so I can't imagine double the capability of the two-years-hence version.

I do have two favourite quotes about change, though. The first is from AD10 from a not particularly insightful or forward-thinking Roman, Sextus Julius Frontinus: 'Man has run out of things to invent'.[2] Although it's easy to make fun of our Roman, in a way, many of us do this – as I say, I can't imagine my phone doubling its capacity. I'm horrified that some say email is dead and we'll all soon communicate by social media alone. I've only just got used to it. It's so seductive to think 'This is as good as it gets' about anything, because we're limited by our imagination.

quote, unquote

Here's another selection of change quotes. Let's get them out of the way. Consider them a gift.

- 'Change imposed is change opposed' (Anonymous).
- 'The universe is change; life is what thinking makes of it' (Marcus Aurelius).
- 'It is said that I am against change. I am not against change. I am in favour of change in the right circumstances. And those circumstances are when it can no longer be resisted' (Paul Johnson in *The Spectator*).
- 'They must often change who would be constant in happiness or wisdom' (Confucius).
- 'You cannot step twice in the same river' (Heraclitus).
- 'Change is not made without inconvenience, even from worse to better' (Richard Hooker).

---

2   He patently didn't see the Corby Trouser Press coming.

Anyway. You get the picture. There are a lot of such quotes. One I do really like, though, and use a lot in my change workshops, is the classic Charles Darwin one:

> It is not the strongest of the species that survives, nor the most intelligent, but the one most responsive to change.

A powerful lesson. If we think back 65 million years to when a big lump of rock hit what was eventually a tequila bar on Mexico's Yucatan Peninsular, it wasn't the biggest or strongest things like the dinosaurs that survived, but the little warm-blooded mouse-type things that were flexible and adaptable and eventually stood upright and became us, and created the need for the Trouser Press.

The corporate world often fails to heed this message. Let's take some fairly recent examples. In 2013, two companies announced that they were in difficulties: HMV and Blockbusters. One of the reasons given in the press was that they didn't see the writing on the wall with regard to the downloading phenomenon; to some extent, they still subscribed to the 'people want to go into shops and browse' model. Which, of course, some do. But not enough anymore.

It doesn't matter how big an organisation you are, or how long-established (HMV has been going since 1921); if the business model doesn't flex and adapt to what people want and/or technological changes, then it's curtains.

And take Nokia. I don't know of many people of a certain age who didn't have a Nokia 3310 phone.[3] It was one of the world's most successful mobile phone brands. But Nokia rested on its laurels, didn't adapt to the meteorite of the smartphone and now appears to have been quietly shelved by its new owners. However, in one of those inevitable twist-of-fate things, as soon as I wrote this I heard they're bringing it back, due to some designer overdosing on irony pills.

leader vs manager

Some writers on change (John Kotter, for example; we'll meet him later) argue that change is the whole thrust behind the leader/manager distinction. Leadership *is* change, according to Kotter. Management is about efficiency in the here and now. It includes such vital competencies as planning, budgeting, organising, problem-solving and managing people. It's really important stuff, and if we don't pay attention to these areas as a manager then we end up being an example of the Peter Principle (people usually get promoted to their level of incompetence).

Leadership is different. It defines what the future should look like,

---

3   Ahh. The days when your battery lasted a week.

determining what should be next on the agenda, and then developing the case for urgency to change the *now* into the *next*. This involves setting strategic direction, creating the inspiring vision and then aligning everyone behind it so they make it happen successfully.[4] It didn't matter how efficiently an individual Blockbusters store was being run if the original business model was flawed.

This is the essence of *transformational* (as opposed to transactional) leadership. Instead of focusing merely on 'stuff', the transformational leader inspires people to reach for the improbable, stirs the emotions and motivates people to buy in to the vision for change.

Management creates predictability and order in the short term. Leadership produces change in the longer term. As Steven Covey puts it, management tells you how to climb the ladder of success. Leadership tells you what wall to lean the ladder against. As I put it in my training, management directs the boat and leadership chooses the port.[5]

what creates change?

The glib answer, I suppose, is what doesn't? But we can be a little more helpful than this. One tool used by change and marketing consultants is the PESTLE analysis, and it's as good a framework as any for thinking through what changes may have an impact on the work of, say, our department or business.

PESTLE analysis

Let's use the university sector as an example.[6] All we do is use the mnemonic PESTLE to think about what *out there* can have an impact on us *in here*.

- **Political**: How does the government of the day view higher education? What about a potential next government? What do they think education is for? How will this impact on the number of places available? What about higher degrees? What about the value placed on research? What about immigration policy with regard to foreign students and academics?
- **Economic**: What impact is the above political landscape likely to have on the funding model? What about the grant vs loan debate and the threshold

---

4   We should add a note of caution here. No matter what level we are in an organisation, we can all demonstrate both managerial and leadership qualities. Leadership is not exclusively for the big cheese.

5   In my experience, they usually drink it as well.

6   The following analysis is for illustrative purposes only and may be completely inaccurate. But then, I'm not in charge of a university.

when loans have to be paid back and the impact this may have on student numbers? What about the wider economy? What about the even wider global economy and its impact on overseas students? What about the possibility of mergers?

- **Social**: What are the social drivers behind going to university? What about the impact of more foreign students studying in the UK? Or, due to Brexit, fewer? What about changes to the way younger people view education? What about demographic changes of both students and staff? What about the impact of student expectations now they are classified (by themselves, if not by most university staff) as fee-paying customers, not students?

- **Technological**: How do students want to learn and on what electronic devices? What about the technological skills of lecturers and the level of IT investment (and therefore support they can get) from internal IT departments? What's the impact on the university if foreign students can access lectures through massive open online courses (MOOCs) and therefore stay in their own country?

- **Legal**: In an increasingly global student economy, what are the legal implications of allowing unlimited – or of limiting – free speech? What about the impact of the Freedom of Information Act? What about the implications of data being compromised? What about changes to human resources laws, such as the end of the default retirement age?

- **Environmental**: What about government policy and sustainability targets? What about the university's green agenda? What about the impact of older buildings on the green agenda? What about property prices or even changing location? What type of environment do students and staff want to study or work in?

So. You get the picture. Try it for yourself. Think about the area (in every sense – physical, sector, profession, department) where you work and then run through the list. You may be surprised at what you think of by having a framework such as PESTLE to work from.

The point is that there are so many factors that can potentially have an impact on your area of work – and you – that the one thing you can be certain of is that things won't stay as they are. And while it's the leader's job to pre-empt this as much as possible by having a vision for where you need to be heading, my argument here is that we're *all* leaders. Don't just leave it up to the people in charge. They may be too busy being managers.

2

the bigger picture

have a vision

In Section 5, we explore how a leader of a team can take their team successfully through change. This change may or may not have been decided by the leader – it could be a diktat from the senior board or the enforced consequence of one or more of the PESTLE considerations,[1] but regardless, it may be your job to implement changes by translating them into what they mean for your team or business area.

Either way, if you take a team through change you have to start with a vision for what it's trying to achieve and what it may look like. What changes do you need to make to ensure you don't go the way of the Nokia 3310? You can't always make such an unlikely comeback. The PESTLE considerations give you the *why*; you need to have a cunning plan to address the *what* and the *how*. We start by thinking about what the future should look like, what our dream is, and what we really care about.

---

1   Or even the result of a dream your boss had after too much cheese. Stranger things have happened.

But we don't work in a vacuum. Unless you're the ultimate Big Boss, you will have a boss. And there'll be an organisational strategy; there may even be a 10-year strategic plan.[2] Whatever you decide to do has to align with whatever's going on organisationally.[3] It's a bit like having your annual appraisal before your boss has theirs; it doesn't make any sense because their appraisal could change everything, and most probably yours.

I do a little exercise with teams to illustrate this point. You get everyone in the team to wander around aimlessly in a big room, looking all casual and random like some kind of human Brownian motion machine, and then shout 'STOP'. Everyone at this point has to stop and, without letting anyone else in the room know, fix two individuals in the room in their mind. Everyone's job is then to try and form – in silence and without letting on who their chosen individuals are – an equilateral triangle with them.

It's really hard, which is sort of the point. Just as you get there, one of your two chosen people moves to form a triangle with someone else. Ad infinitum. It can go on for five minutes. At the debrief, we make the point that this is meant to illustrate the fact that any changes you and your team make have a knock-on effect elsewhere, which may even be hidden from both you and the other teams affected, and eventually come back again to affect your own changes. Ad infinitum.

Having a vision, then, involves identifying what you want to see in the future. You have to care about it. It should fit with your values and be aspirational. But you should want it. Ask yourself questions such as:

- What's the difference between where I want us to be and where we are now?
- What haven't we thought of yet?
- What are the most urgent PESTLE considerations?
- How does this fit with organisational strategy and culture?
- What do I want personally from all this?
- What do I care passionately about?
- What possible future will this open up for me? And my team?
- What does this future look like?
- What will fabulous look like?
- What does my boss want?

---

2   Which half the workforce will think of as a prudent idea and half as a waste of time because of all the potential PESTLE changes.

3   Or at least with what your boss wants.

your own engagement

We may be used to thinking of employee engagement as an abstract concept that involves things such as development and promotional opportunities for staff, informal and formal feedback practices, leadership styles, communication and work-based relationships. The things they ask about in staff surveys.

First of all, though, we have to engage with our own work. When we really feel like we're totally absorbed in our work, using our skills and strengths to achieve stretching targets and meet challenges head on, we enter a state of flow.[4] *Flow* is when we enter a mini time-warp; we look back on a task and think 'That was me on a good day'. I sometimes experience this when presenting to an appreciative audience,[5] or when writing; time flies and the sense of satisfaction and happiness is palpable. This has a knock-on impact on your self-esteem and intrinsic motivation. And, of course, your performance.

We're at our best, then, when we enjoy what we do and the way we do it. When we work in accordance with our key skills, strengths and motivational drivers, we bring our best selves to work. Add to this our vision for the future, our own career or managerial aspirations and some clarity of whatever direction our team or organisation needs to head in, and we are being leaders.

There's another reason why this is important. Again, Section 5 expands on this but if you don't have engagement, it's really difficult to help your teams have it. Emotions leak. When you're the boss, however, multiply the leakage by a factor of 10.

your team's engagement

Engagement is therefore partly about the impact you have on your team and colleagues. Get this right and you become a catalyst for creative thinking about the future of your area, and you draw to you those who connect with your vision and want to be a part of it. Ultimately, it's all about relationships. Leadership is a relational thing; management is a process thing. We need both.

This is why command-and-control is fine in an emergency, but ultimately has a shelf-life. It doesn't create engagement. If we carry on being directive after the emergency, we tend to be met with apathy, grudging compliance or outright resistance. My first book (*The Psychological Manager: Improve Your*

---

4   Made famous by Csikszentmihalyi. I don't know either.

5   Yes, it does occasionally happen.

Performance Conversations) explored this concept. Here's what I said (on p 105):

> ... *command-and-control doesn't really work that well with adults, as many dictators have found. We don't remember things as effectively when we're told, as opposed to when we've experienced them for ourselves. We don't perform to goals as readily when they are imposed. If we accept that a manager's job is to get the task done and retain/grow their team, then coaching hits both spots. It's not always the best approach (pure knowledge transfer when time is of the essence is not a recipe for a coaching conversation) but it is a great one for your toolkit. And one in which you learn, too. Win/win.*

In that book, I explore the key concepts of people management; having the attitude that it's an important part of the day job, understanding how to motivate your staff, setting great stretching goals with your team and giving excellent constructive feedback on the results. We really turn up the dial on your people management skills by suggesting that creating a coaching culture is one of the most effective ways in which we create engagement. And creating engagement helps the change process. We create the vision; then inspire our teams to work towards it through really good people management.

organisational engagement

A discussion on engagement isn't complete without mentioning the bigger picture of organisational engagement. As we've said, your team doesn't work in a vacuum. The MacLeod Report to government (November 2012) was in response to the perception that there was an engagement gap in the UK; people weren't as committed to their organisation's goals and values as they could be – and had maybe lost the link with this and their own sense of wellbeing.[6]

The report suggested a causal link with productivity – that low engagement correlates with low performance. This obviously passes the common sense test[7] but the authors claim hard evidence[8] and suggest that increasing employee engagement should be – and is – a key priority for UK leaders. It impacts on performance and productivity as we mentioned, but also

---

6   In the survey, only one-third of UK workers said they were engaged at work.

7   If not falling foul of the 'No shit, Sherlock' school of research.

8   Of the world's most admired companies, 94% believe that their efforts to engage their employees have created a competitive advantage (Hay); the top 25% of organisations (in terms of high employee engagement levels) had twice the annual income and returned seven times more to shareholders over a five-year period than the bottom 25%; Marks and Spencer's own research showed that those stores with a focus on improving engagement levels delivered £62 million more sales every year than those with declining engagement. You get the picture.

absenteeism, staff retention, levels of innovation, customer service and on positive outcomes in public services.

The MacLeod Report identified four enablers of engagement – and this is where we start to see the link with creating successful change. While the report relates to the bigger-picture, whole-organisation level – and as such needs to be role-modelled and reinforced right from the very top – it contains lessons for every leader of every team. Bear these four enablers of engagement in mind when we get to Section 5. To be honest they're common sense, but unfortunately it's pretty rare for them to be specifically addressed.

four enablers of engagement

These are:

- Having visible, empowering leadership providing a strong strategic narrative about the organisation, where it's come from and where it's going.
- Having engaging managers who focus on their people and give them scope, treat them as individuals and coach and stretch them.
- Having an employee voice throughout the organisation, for reinforcing and challenging views; between functions and externally. Employees are seen as central to the solution.
- Having organisational integrity – the values on the wall are reflected in day-to-day behaviours – with no 'say-do' gap.

We reinforce many of these concepts when we look at managing successful change in your own teams. Your team will want to know the narrative of the change – the story of what it looks like – and what it means for them. They'll have to be (and if you're an excellent line manager,[9] will want to be) stretched and coached. You have to see them as part of the solution, not the problem. And you need to role-model what you want to see behaviourally.

organisational culture

Of course, all of this engagement and visioning can be overridden (or underpinned) by the prevailing culture of your particular organisation. The oft-styled management guru Peter Drucker once said 'Culture eats strategy for breakfast', and by that he means that in whatever strategic direction you want to take an organisation (or by inference, your team or department), its success

---

9 Or have read my first book. It's really rather good.

will be determined by whether the culture supports it or not. Culture triumphs in the organisational top trumps card deck.

It doesn't need to be as black and white as McGregor's concept of dividing managers (and an organisation's culture) into 'People are lazy workshy fops and need coercing into performing' (Theory X) or 'People just need the encouragement and then will naturally seek meaningful, challenging and stretching work' (Theory Y).

Culture is ultimately more complex.[10] It's pretty much defined as 'The way we do things around here', and being helped into understanding and finding your way around a brand new organisation culturally has a massive impact on attrition rates in the first six months of employment. This is why organisational mentoring schemes or buddying programmes are such good value.

Culture is the by-product of a variety of influences. The organisation's history, for example. The beliefs and values of its founder members. To some extent, its structure and location(s). Its sector. Changing this culture is usually really, really hard.[11]

Let's go back to the concept of flow. This is what we need organisationally – a culture of flow – if our organisation is going to be one of engagement. It may be that we have to start small – creating a culture of flow within our own teams first and see who notices. You may just find people start wanting a bit of it themselves. Whether it's the whole organisation or your part of it, creating a culture of flow requires some key elements:

- Ensure you demonstrate best practice in goal-setting and constructive, coaching-style feedback.[12]
- Provide appropriate challenge to match individual skill. In other words, keep people challenged but not too much.
- Try to keep distractions from the key tasks to a minimum. People will get deeply involved in their task, and too many distractions reduces their focus.
- Allow your people autonomy and independence – give them control.

Big culture-change projects usually fail.[13] Depressing, but there you go. The reasons are many and complex and we address some of these later, but one

---

10   I have, however, worked in what felt like a predominantly Theory X culture. It wasn't pleasant. I didn't survive.

11   Think banking. What gets measured, gets done. That'll be profits, then.

12   If only there was a book that could help you. Ooo, I know! *The Psychological Manager: Improve Your Performance Conversations*. That one.

13   According to McKinsey & Co, at least two-thirds of them do.

of the main reasons is that they're treated like an IT implementation project (nothing wrong with that) with spreadsheets and Gant charts and everything, forgetting that the changes have to be undertaken by real people who need to be engaged and behave in accordance with the changes (plenty wrong with that). Cultural change is the end point of the transformation process, and in big organisations it can take up to five years.

Kotter's model

John Kotter thought he had the answer. His analysis was based on watching (or being involved with) 15 years' worth of organisations failing in their change projects. His starting point echoes the gist of Section 2 of this book; that change is painful and most of us don't like it, so most of us resist it.

So Kotter worked out why the particular change initiatives he observed had failed, and came up with an eight-stage model to address each one: the antidote, if you like, to each of the eight reasons why big cultural-change projects fail.

stage 1: establish the sense of urgency

People don't like change. They often resist it. Or are in denial about its need. So we're going nowhere if we fail to jolt people out of their comfortable complacency. Which very much includes management, by the way. The need for change is often underestimated, or the focus is on short-term profit, not long-term success – or otherwise.[14] People need to be convinced – from the board down; if you're profitable now, why the need for change? I'll let the names Blockbusters and HMV roll around your unconscious until Section 2.

Consultants are often used to do the convincing – the organisation can metaphorically shoot the messenger, then reluctantly and begrudgingly agree with the findings and blame the consultant.[15] As an illustration of this, a few years ago the CEOs of some US car firms went cap-in-hand to government, asking for money. In their private jets. It was duly commented on that they were hardly creating the sense of urgency. One congressman asked specifically why they hadn't jet-pooled! Kotter suggests that the sense of urgency can be ramped up by creating a financial crisis, eliminating obvious examples of excess (like a jet, for example) or even setting unreachable targets.

---

14 The university sector has been accused of this. Because of the time lag (students already booked on to courses, the vagaries of the funding model, etc) the impact of the 2009 recession hit them later than it did industry, and yet still seemed to catch some of them by surprise.

15 'Don't look at us! The big guns made us do it.'

stage 2: form a powerful guiding coalition

While the initial impetus behind the cultural transformation may be led by just a few people (or even just the CEO), a successful large change needs a core team whose job it is to focus on the change. This group needs to be seen as an autonomous unit with a high degree of trust, and a shared objective that appeals to both head and heart. This team needs to be credible (not driven by HR, although they should be represented) and its members should have enough power and expertise – as well as individuals with strong leadership qualities.

stage 3: create the vision

Once again, we're back to vision. A clear vision must be established that appeals to all likely stakeholders: management, staff and customers. It should be a pull into the future to counter the push of Stage 1 – motivational, aspirational and positive. It should address the *why* and start to address the *what*; leaving the *how* to local devices to avoid claims of dictatorial micromanagement. It's the direction of travel that's to be determined here: simple, clear, powerful. Without it, people won't understand why they have to go through short-term pain to get to long-term gain. As Kotter himself puts it:

> *A good vision acknowledges that sacrifices will be necessary but makes clear that these sacrifices will yield particular benefits and personal satisfactions that are far superior to those available today – or tomorrow – without attempting to change.*

It aligns people: we're all in this together and going in *this* direction.

stage 4: communicate the vision

In every way possible. Use technology such as chat rooms and wikis, websites and email. Use meetings and roadshows with the help of Marketing or Internal Communications teams. Most organisations cascade to middle management and hold them to account for having meaningful change-based conversations.

And then communicate some more.[16] It needs to be simple, using metaphor and analogy and examples; it also needs to be repeated often in a variety of formats, and role-modelled from the top. And as good communication is always two-way, concerns and opinions need to be listened to: remember the four enablers of engagement!

---

16 Whenever I do a team diagnosis, a team build or a 360 degree feedback project, communication is the number one gripe. Every single time.

stage 5: empower others to act on the vision

There's no point in an organisation attempting some big cultural change if the systems, processes and structures aren't aligned – or if they work contrary to the vision. If an organisation wants to improve its cross-team collaboration, then it not only needs to notice and reward such behaviours, but also needs to change anything that gets in the way (such as an internal funding model based on competition). You have to help people to behave in accordance with the shift in culture you want. In addition, people who are blockers to the change need to be brought on board. We look at how to do this in Section 5.

stage 6: generate short-term wins

Culture change takes time. A long time. So long that some argue that it's easier and more effective to just work with what you have and nudge it. It's really hard for people to stay focused and keep the momentum and motivation for change going for prolonged periods, so you need to build in and celebrate milestones along the way. These wins need to be clearly related, unambiguously, to the bigger change effort.

stage 7: consolidating improvements

This means, effectively, don't declare victory too soon, as forward momentum will stop. If the changes already built are not fully bedded in, the danger is that the organisation – or, more accurately, the people in it – will slip back to the old ways. The guiding coalition (see Stage 2) needs to build on the credibility gained from the short-term wins, and make bigger changes.

stage 8: institutionalising the new

This is about anchoring the new ways of behaving so they become the new normal. This is about good old-fashioned performance management and the setting of behavioural expectations, and also about helping individuals to explicitly see the benefits of the changes. And, no doubt, further nudges will also be needed to build on the change effort and to make *change* the new normal.

If we can bring this back to the individual level,[17] we need to be lifelong learners, according to Kotter. Original models of change, such as that of Kurt Lewin in the 1940s, talked about change being a three-stage process: unfreeze

---

17 It's amazing that we can so easily fall into the trap of conceptualising an organisation as a thing in itself, with a personality and motivations. It's usually just a building or two with people in. The culture becomes the sum total of the people, practices and systems. But ultimately, it's just people.

the old, tinker about a bit, then refreeze the new. The problem is, it never quite refreezes anymore, if indeed it ever did.

So as the world stays stubbornly slushy, we therefore have to be more tolerant of ambiguity. As we cover in Section 2, most of us find this rather uncomfortable for all sorts of biological, neurological and evolutionary reasons. Kotter argues that we need to break ourselves out of this craving for order and become habitual self-aware risk-takers, being open to new ideas and essentially embracing change. It appears that most of us still have some way to go.

appreciative enquiry

I'd like to mention one more model before we move on to the really interesting brain stuff. It's not a model of culture change per se, but rather a way of determining what needs to change and what existing strengths our organisation or team have that we need to keep.[18] Most change models (like the Kotter one) tend to start with what the problem is, what's going wrong or what needs to change. At an individual level, this is what clumsy appraisal processes can make us feel like – negative, drained of energy and like we don't quite cut the mustard.

A different way of looking at change is to identify what already works well that you want to keep, and then build on this by turning up the dial on these things. There are many writers on organisational culture (Kotter among them) who argue that it's best to try to work with what you have and nudge, rather than go for big culture change – because as we've already seen, big culture change is really hard and often fails.

This methodology is called *appreciative enquiry*, and its principle is pretty simple. If we spend time and energy focusing on what's currently going well, it generates more positive energy and enthusiasm, and – as we see later – this tends to generate more solutions because we're not merely in survival mode. The process is all about asking the right powerful questions, and creating an atmosphere of curiosity and a willingness to take a step back and view the organisation or team through a new lens.

For it to work, you need to try to 'Get the whole organisation in the room' as one of the founders of the process, David Cooperrider, suggests, because all bits link to all the other bits. At an organisational level, this can be a logistical nightmare, although Cooperrider himself has used the technique with nearly 1,000

18   There's a real parallel with dealing with change at an individual level here which we'll see in Sections 4 and 5, all of which come from the Positive Psychology movement.

participants. For most of us, getting together a selection of interested stakeholders (more on this in Section 5) and the creative use of technology may help.

The starting point is to determine the positive future that you want to create – not the problem you want to solve, which is the more usual way. This works with goal-setting theory, too – you're far more likely to achieve results if you develop goals that move you towards something, rather than away or stopping something. It feels different and generates a solution-mindset.

the four Ds

Once you know what the future could be, there are four stages to the process:

- **Discovery**: This is about identifying processes or behaviours that already work well. Participants often tell stories (tapping into the way our brains are wired – to understand the world through narrative) about successes, key qualities, resources, talents or strengths that your team or organisation has.
- **Dream**: What might be? What does a glorious future look like, sound like, feel like? This is about taking the Discovery stories and projecting them into the future to the brave new world that you want to create. How can things be even better? How precisely is it different from now? What will you be noticing? How will people be behaving?
- **Design**: This is about identifying how we get there. The important thing is to keep the focus on the positive and not get sucked into problem-solving. What needs to stay the same? What needs to change? How can we do this? What systems can support the new behaviours? Who else needs to be involved?
- **Destiny**: This final stage is about implementing the plan – when the dream becomes a reality. Focusing on the positive again is vital here, the argument being that people will become naturally energised and will work towards this new future because they have passion for it. There's no one way to achieve this, and since the positive changes will create more positive changes, a change champion or project leader may help keep everything on track.

Appreciative enquiry, then, is perhaps more a model of how to create the energy to make the change stick rather than the more process- and solution-driven approach of writers like John Kotter.

In Section 5, we look at a model of taking a team through change that in many ways builds on both of these models, but is more practical and immediately implementable at a team level. It also takes into account all the exciting biology bits that we discuss next: why we react to change in the way that we do.

section 1 summary:
the context of change

This section aims to reinforce the message that change is inevitable, due to the huge number of factors that are destined to stop things always staying the same. Some writers call the rise of the internet the new Industrial Revolution, and its impact is already no less radical. There's more computing power in your smartphone than in enough 1970s' mainframe computers to fill a small building.

When looking at change in our own area – change that affects our jobs, for example – it's useful to think of the wider context: the vision of the leadership, your organisation's striving for engagement and the overriding culture of the organisation. Kotter's model of taking a whole organisation through a major cultural change may be beyond our own particular remit, but we can and should learn why change projects are usually less than successful. We return to some of these themes in Section 5, when we look at taking your own team through change.

key learning points

1. Change is the only constant. There. I've said it.
2. It's our flexibility and adaptability that help us to survive – as an individual and as an organisation.
3. Management is about maintaining the status quo; leadership is about change.
4. We should be both managers and leaders.
5. A PESTLE analysis can help us to determine what factors can make change inevitable.
6. Any change starts with a vision – what the future should look like.
7. When we're fully engaged as individuals, we can experience a state of *flow* – us on a good day!
8. Managing your team's engagement (and ultimately managing change) builds on excellent people- and performance-management skills, such as goal-setting, understanding motivation, giving constructive feedback, coaching and team building.
9. The four enablers of engagement at an organisational level are obviously related: having visible, empowering leadership; having engaging people managers with the requisite skills; having a strong employee voice throughout the organisation; and having organisational integrity.
10. Ultimately, culture trumps any strategic direction. Every time.

exercises

1. Do your own PESTLE analysis (Appendix 1) on your organisation, and another one on your department or team. Are they different? What changes need to happen? How ready is your organisation to deal with these potential drivers for change? How ready are you?

2. How would you describe the culture of your organisation? How would you describe the culture of your department or team? Again, are they different? Does it help or hinder your organisation's (or department or team's) objectives? What needs to change?

3. Summarise this by performing a SWOT analysis (Appendix 2: Strengths, Weaknesses, Opportunities, Threats) on your organisation and again on your department or team. Is there anything here that surprises you?

4. To what extent are you able to describe your organisation's vision? What about its values? How much congruence is there with your own?

5. Write your own change quote. One you actually believe in.[19]

---

19   Here's mine: 'Nothing much changes, apart from everything.'

how (and why) we react to change

'We must die to one life before we can enter into another'

Anatole France

3

a step back in time

lights, camera, action!

Picture the scene. It's 60,000 years ago and you're sitting there in your hunter/gatherer cave in what will eventually be Essex. You're calm, relaxed, feeling secure in your surroundings and the company of your tribe, when all of a sudden you notice a change in the atmosphere. Your senses pick it up before you fully realise what's going on; your hearing's suddenly heightened and the hairs stand up on the back of your neck. Something isn't right.

Then, out of the corner of your eye, you see in the cave entrance the unmistakeable shape of a sabre-toothed cat.[1] Along with the rest of your tribe your reactions are phenomenally quick. Your heart beats more quickly to get blood to where it's needed, and you breathe quickly and shallowly to get a rush of oxygen. You grab your spear and with your compatriots rush towards the source of danger in as threatening a way as possible – and chase the cat away.

---

1   No doubt pretty miffed at being downgraded from a tiger. Actually, we met him in my first book, *The Psychological Manager: Improve Your Performance Conversations* (p 36).

There's a reason why we react like this, of course. It's quick. In the normal measurement of human (and we were pretty much human by then) reactions, it's virtually instantaneous. And in immediate danger like in this scenario, 'quick' wins over 'considered' every time. It's the classic *fight/flight* reaction and those that had it survived to tell the tale and no doubt used it as a chat-up line to help further the species and ensure the survival of the process.[2]

Feeling an emotion, such as fear in the example above, then reacting, is quick. Thinking about something and deciding what course of action to take is slow. So we learned to do both. And most of the time it works. If it didn't, evolution no doubt would've had something to say – and then done something about it.

The quick mode (Daniel Kahneman (*Thinking, Fast and Slow*) calls it system 1, or Thinking Fast) helps us now when we see an angry face and we instinctively know how to respond, or at least puts us on our guard. It's there when we dive into a canal to save someone or push someone out of the way of a falling piano. Thinking about it takes longer – at least five times longer – so we developed a bypass system for emergencies.

our brain. it's a bit weird

Our brain is essentially a three-pound mass of jelly-like cells that convert the 'out there' into some sort of reality. The 'real' world as such has no sound, or colour, but our brains construct these things in our head so we can live in it. I know this sounds a bit weird and is a throwback to the 'If a tree falls in the forest and there's no-one to hear it, how many badgers does it kill' or whatever the saying is.

It's the truth, though. All sound is, for example, is a stream of air molecules hitting your eardrum, converting the vibration into noise that the brain interprets as sound. No brain, no noise. The upshot of this, of course, as this works for all our perceptual mechanisms, is that reality is personal to us and made up. All of our senses depend on the others – our sight affects our hearing, our smell affects our taste and so, surprisingly, does our sight. Sight leads to an expectation of taste.

Try this test (this has been done by a wine-expert friend of mine and also in published psychological tests). Chill two glasses of wine, one red and one white, to the same temperature. Blindfold yourself. Get a friend to pass you one of the glasses. Even wine experts can't tell the difference once they don't know

---

2   Presumably those that said 'Ooo, look at this stripy orange and black thing with big teeth and everything! I wonder what that does?' didn't live long enough to find out, and certainly not long enough to pass on their genes.

whether it's red or white. Expectation affects taste.[3]

Even our perception of time is a bit dodgy. We live half a second in the past. It takes that long to perceive things, so by the time you notice anything, it's already been and gone. The upshot of all this is that the bit of reality we perceive is determined by the brain structures we have in place for noticing it. It's only a bit of what's 'out there'. X-rays and ultraviolet light are out there, but we wouldn't know it because we don't have the right bits to notice them. In the case of ultraviolet light, bees know about it because they do.

The final nail in the coffin of our concept of reality is that all of our perceptions, memories and attention first pass through the filter of our beliefs and values, which come from our already existing versions of reality, which in turn are based on our upbringing. This is important because many of the remedies for a lack of resilience (Section 4) are based on this concept. The first step is recognising that all anything is, ever, is a made-up interpretation of it, based on a fraction of the evidence and drained through the sieve of our belief systems.

At the time of writing, therefore, there are something like seven billion different versions of reality on the planet. When I was born in the early 1960s, there were about three billion versions. That means that the world is just a bit more than double as weird as when I was born.

so who, actually, are we?

So, what makes us *us*, then? We don't come as hardwired as a meerkat. We're far more of a blank slate, which means we're helpless for a lot longer but also have the luxury and capability of creating things.[4] We tend to learn on the job; by the time we're two years old, each of our neurons (we discuss these later in this section) has around 15,000 connections, but then we start to lose them and keep (and reinforce) the important ones. This process affects what we learn, what we notice and who we, as an individual, become.

Our memories are constructed using this process, but the problem with memory is that it changes after the event. We don't have the equivalent of a hard-drive recorder in our head. We have a forever-changing interpretation of the event, although that's not how it feels. Later memories change and even

---

3 The outcome of this research means that there's no point buying anything other than the House wine at a restaurant if you train yourself to expect it to be just as good. Unless it's Blue Nun, of course.

4 Such as toy meerkats. Or a trouser press.

override earlier ones.[5] Even our memories, then, are a myth.

The other bit that feels like us is our consciousness. There are whole books devoted to this subject and we still don't really know what it is, but most writers in this area seem to agree that it emerges from the integration – and as a sort of by-product – of all the other bits of the brain, so it can work as one. David Eagleman, a prolific writer on the subject, likens this to the CEO of an organisation: the CEO is there to join the dots between all the bits and decide the direction of travel for the organisation; likewise, consciousness does the same thing for us. It helps all the bits work in sync. According to most neuroscientists, consciousness is therefore a by-product of having a lot of component parts. Develop an artificial brain powerful enough, then theoretically at least – according to some neuroscientists – consciousness could spontaneously emerge.

And what's the point? Our consciousness helps us to deal with the unexpected by making various parts of the brain work together to deal with threat or potential opportunity. It rises out of the detail and takes the long view. It's the brain's leader.

brain structure: the old bit

the hindbrain

Let's go back to our sabre-toothed cat scenario again. The process we described there is reflected in how our brains are structured. The oldest bit of the brain, evolutionarily-speaking, is the bit at the top of our spinal cord with parts called, variously, the hindbrain, the cerebellum, the reptilian brain, brain stem or Reticular Activating System, if we want to be clever.

This part of the brain keeps us alive when we're not thinking about staying alive – but more importantly for our purposes, it acts as our first filter on the world. It effectively says to the next bit of the brain 'You'd better pay attention to this, it may be important'. Some writers refer rather unkindly to this part of the brain as asking three questions of any change in the environment: can I eat it? can it eat me? and can I mate with it?[6] Anyway – its function is to notice change, and if it detects it, to pass on the information to the next part of the

---

5   The fallibility of memory to manipulation was famously demonstrated by psychologist Elizabeth Loftus, who's done a huge amount of research into eyewitness testimony. Two groups of people are shown the same video image of two cars crashing. One group is asked to estimate the speed one of the cars is travelling as it hits the other (stationary) one; the other group is asked the same question, worded 'How fast is the car travelling as it *smashes* into the stationary one'. The two groups remembered different speeds, despite watching the same video.

6   Not necessarily always in that order.

brain. If things haven't changed, this probably didn't hurt us, so to this bit of the brain it makes sense to focus on new things that might hurt us.

This is important for the theme of this book. This 200,000-year-old (at least) system is still with us – we effectively have the same hardware – and so this part of our brain is continuously scanning our environment for threat or opportunity. It's on the lookout for whatever our sabre-toothed cat equivalent is nowadays, and our response – a fight/flight response – may not be the most appropriate, even if we are still in Essex.

As an example of the vestiges this bit of the brain has left us with, consider moving in a car or on a rolling cross-channel ferry. This bit of the brain tells you that you're moving, and can't tell that you aren't just because your legs aren't. Your sense of balance, determined through the fluids in your inner ear, doesn't think so. There's a mismatch of signals, and the result is you feeling unwell. To your hindbrain, this means one thing: poison. So it makes you say hello to your breakfast again to get rid of it. Your hindbrain did not evolve to deal with a P&O ferry.

It's easy to see why we need this primary filter on the world. There are billions of bits and bytes of data flying around us at any given moment and we can't possibly pay attention to all of it, so it filters out what isn't that important. This system therefore tells us what *is* important by focusing on change. If there appears to be a material change, as gleaned often unconsciously through our senses,[7] then the information gets through the filter to the next bit of the brain.

It's emotional.

brain structure: the next oldest bit

the limbic system

Or at least part of it is. The middle part of the brain again has a few working parts, but collectively it's often called the limbic system and comprises largely our memory bank (the hippocampus – effectively our hard drive), the thalamus and hypothalamus (memory relay stations and primary drive regulation, respectively) and the amygdala.

The amygdala is important and we revisit its role in the section on emotional intelligence, but for now we can think of it as our second filter and where our brain catalogues emotional memories. It is responsive to the classic threat responses we discussed above, and will start a stress response that

---

7   Interestingly, it appears that smell is the one sense that doesn't pass through this part of the brain, but rather has a direct hotline to emotion.

eventually leads to the fight/flight mechanism being invoked. Not only that – it actively releases hormones that stop the more logical parts of the brain from functioning, because survival is more important than being right.

This system works in tandem and very quickly. Your hippocampus remembers what a sabre-toothed cat is, and your amygdala knows how to respond based on emotional memory from the past, or from similar transferable situations that it's reminded of. It doesn't do subtlety. When we have a seemingly irrational reaction to someone we've never met before and feel we just don't like them, one possible explanation is that this system is remembering someone else from your past and you're having the emotional reaction driven by your amygdala transposed on to them. This could also be the root of some phobias.

This limbic system, then, creates the stress response attributed to our sabre-toothed cat invasion by releasing the stress chemical norepinephrine to prepare the body immediately for attack. In a way, the amygdala acts as our second filter, as it stops the brain from thinking. Thinking is slow (system 2, according to Kahneman), and time may be of the essence. We have, therefore, what's called an amygdala-hijack or limbic system overload, and our response is an emotional one based on survival. No room – or time – for thought.

And one of the reasons why we all react slightly differently to change or other stressful situations is that what's stored by our amygdala as emotional memories depends on our own past events, culture and upbringing. It also appears that the amount of perceived control we have over the situation causing the overload has a large impact on this limbic system arousal, which gives us a remedy – we can choose, with practice, to think about things differently.

This system can be amazingly quick. Researchers in Sweden found that people reacted (by generating a sweaty palm) to pictures of snakes when the image was shown for less than 1\300th of a second. As it takes nearly half a second to consciously perceive the image, the participants were in effect responding to things before they saw them. We might label this 'intuition', of course.

Interestingly, the olfactory system (which detects and recognises smell) is part of this limbic system. This is why smells are often associated with powerful emotional memories, aided by the fact that the olfactory bulb and the hippocampus are pretty much next to each other. How we label the smell can also affect our experience of it: one well-known experiment found that people determined whether a smell was pleasant or unpleasant after smelling it simply by the label – 'Christmas tree' or 'Toilet cleaner', for example – taking us back to our wine story!

brain structure: the new bit

the neocortex and lobes

The final part of the brain is the bit that makes us 'human'. It consists of grey matter (our neocortex: five millimetres thick, the size of a tea towel and folded around our brain so it can fit in) and white matter. The two types of matter combine in various structures called lobes (four pairs, one in each hemisphere) to form the thinking part of the brain.

There are lobes that store visual memories and process visual stimuli (occipital lobes), those that do the same for auditory information and auditory memory (temporal lobes) and those that deal more with spatial awareness and perception (parietal lobes). More importantly, for our purposes, the fourth pair is responsible for planning, judgement, decision-making and creativity. This is our frontal lobe and prefrontal cortex – the bit behind our forehead that hurts when we think a lot.

This was the last bit of the brain to develop in evolutionary terms, and is also the last bit to develop as we progress through childhood and young adulthood – our ability to logically reason and understand risk seems to peak at the age of 23 or so with the full development of our frontal lobe. After then it's just fine-tuning.[8] This is also the only part of our brain that can control emotions – one of its functions is therefore to control the impulses of the amygdala. Without it, we wouldn't be able to control urges or solve problems or make decisions. As this bit was the last to evolve, it didn't hold us back when we 'decided' to come down from the trees, and certainly didn't worry about the lack of trouser presses.

An awful lot of our decisions aren't exactly, erm, decisions. Sometimes we have a hunch, or intuition about something – this is merely the various bits of the brain noticing things before the conscious mind does. Remember, our prefrontal cortex is often playing catch-up. Sometimes our bodies notice and respond to things without our being entirely aware of it. In one study (I'll let you decide whether it was gratuitous or not) psychologists found that lap-dancers earned more tips when they were ovulating, as men pick up on the subtle bodily clues without being aware of it.[9] This prompted the men to find them more attractive as potential (fertile) mates.

Some decisions may even have genetic roots. One of the 'Big Five' personality variables (see Chapter 8) is *Openness to Experience*, which may have some

---

8   Practising brain-training games helps you get better at brain-training games. Nothing else.

9   Psychologists. How we suffer for our science.

genetic markers and helps create a more liberal political persuasion. Our politics may have a genetic root. Likewise, the strength of our disgust response (to images of rotting corpses, for example) correlates with a more conservative outlook politically. Some argue that our over-arching political bias is therefore a function of our DNA! This doesn't mean that we can't change it – as we'll see, eventually we can change any belief system – it's just that it's hard, so we tend not to.

Finally, this frontal lobe contains our chief executive: the prefrontal cortex. It receives information from pretty much everywhere else, sends out commands and is our primary decision-making structure. It therefore tries to make sense of all the separate bits of information and sensory input, and make decisions as to how to think or act. In a way, as we've already seen, it is the seat of our consciousness.

brain structure: putting it all together

This description of the brain is, of course, grossly simplified.[10] But even this simplistic explanation of its structure helps us to understand something quite profound. Our brain is geared to notice and react to change as if it's a threat. It therefore creates an emotional response to this threat before it even gets to our prefrontal cortex and starts actually thinking about it. We can eventually route it through the logic, rationality and decision-making areas of the brain, but it takes a lot longer and we don't always have time.

This really helped when we had to be mindful of stripy cave invaders, and is still useful when we face an attack or dodge an errant shopping trolley, but the same mechanism is potentially invoked when we face a stroppy customer or an angry email from the boss. More generally, however, it's often the process behind our reaction to all kinds of change in our home or professional lives. Essentially, we operate in survival mode and that comes at a cost – poorer decision-making, poorer interpersonal skills and poorer emotional control.

how we learn

So, we've described the basic structure of the brain and how this all works through a sequence of processes when we notice a change in our environment. The implications for how we deal with change in general terms may be becoming clear, but before we look at this there's one more process to discuss – how we learn.

---

10 I love the saying that if the brain were simple enough for us to understand it, we'd be too simple to understand it. It also seems to try to avoid being studied, which is just rude.

Our brains are made up of a particular type of cell, called a neuron. Its job is pretty simple: to form connections. We have around 100 billion of these cells[11] and it used to be thought (as late as the 1990s) that we were unable to generate new ones. But we now know that learning something new not only forces new connections, but also creates new brain cells in a process called neurogenesis. The brain is far more malleable – or plastic – then we ever thought, and we actually physically change our brain by what we think and the way we think, as we generate new cells and connections through purposeful practice – self-directed neuroplasticity, if you're interested. Reading this book is changing your brain physically.

neurons and how they work

The neuron's job, then, is to talk to other neurons. Each neuron has three main parts – the cell body, dendrites (which are like a set of filaments coming from the cell body) and the main stem of the neuron, the axon. If you imagine an eyeball on a stalk, you're not far off.[12] The gap between the cells (between the end of one axon and the dendrites of the next neuron – or more accurately, thousands of others) is called a synapse.

The process works like this. The neuron sending the signal to talk to the next neuron releases a chemical that changes the amount of electricity in that cell, which then travels down the axon. Axons are covered by a fatty substance called a myelin sheath that aids the transmission of the signal – we get this from omega 3 (among other things), which is why fish is considered brain food.[13] When the signal gets to the end of the axon, it releases chemicals called neurotransmitters, which swim across the synaptic gap and are taken up by the dendrites of another neuron.

These dendrites grow as we learn and are pared back when we don't, so as we learn and think, our brains change. The more times we repeat the thought or behaviour (a B minor guitar chord or the French word for red) then the impulse sequence through the neurons is repeated until it becomes hardwired into a network of cells that get used to firing together.

Many parts of the brain can 'learn' to fire together through this process

---

11   Interestingly, we have more of these cells in our stomach than a cat does in its head. Which says a lot about cats. This has been used as an explanation for the existence of 'gut feelings' – and also the stupidity of cats. (I may be giving away personal feelings here.)

12   And 10,000 biologists put their heads in their hands.

13   But not the night before an exam. It's a little late by then.

to complete a specific task – Hebb's law states 'Cells that fire together, wire together'. All a memory is, when you think of it like this, is a sequence of firing synapses, not the neurons themselves. It's the sequence that holds the memory, called encoding. And, of course, unlike a computer, our perceptions and existing memories affect the new one and therefore change it. As we've said, memory is constructed after the event – it's not a digital recording. The result of this is that nothing you remember is ever 'real', for any given definition of real. You made it up. Or rather, your brain did.

neurotransmitters

It's worth spending a little time thinking about the neurotransmitters – the chemicals that jump the gap between neurons and forge connections. Some neurotransmitters cause a neuron to send a message to another cell, while some stop it from firing. There are dozens of neurotransmitters, but some of the most important for our purposes are:

*   norepinephrine (also called noradrenaline, which affects our moods and triggers the stress response)
*   serotonin (enhances mood and calms us)
*   endorphins (the brain's natural painkiller, often generated by social contact and laughing)
*   dopamine (assists with focus).

An important one that's both a hormone and a neurotransmitter is oxytocin – the 'you are my friend' chemical. This gives you that lovely feeling when you're in love or lust, or feel a close bond with a significant other. This seems to have been important in helping us to bond as a tribe back in that Essex cave by suppressing norepinephrine (the stress chemical), which is normally a more sensible survival response to anyone not in your tribe. I've written about this before in *The Psychological Manager: Improve Your Performance Conversations* (p 137), and the impact this process has on teams and our natural tendency for silo-working. It is, in effect, the science behind ingroup vs outgroup. HR vs Finance. Arsenal vs Tottenham.

When we exercise, or take anti-depressants, or eat certain foods, or have social interaction, or receive praise, *or go through change*, our brain's chemistry changes at the neurotransmitter level. This affects how we feel. Which affects our thoughts. Which affect our behaviour.

We return to this model later on, but it's useful to have an idea of the science behind it as this helps us to have more control over it. And when we have more control, we have more options for how we deal with change. This process is at play when we learn a language or a skill – but it's also how we learn to deal with our emotions and behavioural responses to those emotions.

4

what this all means

All of this – our evolutionary history, our brain structure and the way we learn – means something quite profound. Our first reaction to change, which our brain tends to perceive as a threat, is emotional, not rational. The result is the classic *change curve*.

the change curve

Now everyone is different and every situation is different. But our responses to change and life's stressful events tend to have some commonalities. So much work has been done in this area that it's almost passed into folklore, but essentially our classic response to change, heavily influenced by the way our brains work, is fairly predictable.

shock

First, there's typically shock, followed by a period of flat affect – numbness. Essentially, our brains find it difficult to comprehend what's going on and therefore go into buffer mode. This may be fleeting or may last for several days, as our thoughts keep on repeating the circumstances that led to the shock.

denial

This is often followed by a period of denial – or even a sense of false optimism and heightened mood! This is our brain's way of putting us into a holding pattern. The event may be just too enormous to deal with right now, so our brain goes into protection mode and for a while pretends it isn't happening, allowing us to regroup and gather the energy to deal with it. It's amazing how long we can last in this denial phase, and how illogical it appears to an observer. People still turn up for work long after being made redundant. We set a place for dinner for someone who's no longer with us. We steadfastly ignore all the warning signs of an impending change and yet are somehow surprised and shocked when it happens.

Of course, sometimes the change may be made up of small incremental changes or nudges that are harder to spot on their own. A frog may allow itself to be boiled alive if you very gradually increase the temperature of the water.[1] But regardless, our capacity for both conscious and unconscious denial is greater than most of us realise. Denial is not bad in itself – it puts things off until we can deal with them – but long term, it can have a dramatic impact[2] if we don't eventually accept the event and go through the rest of the change curve.

anxiety and anger

And that's when it hits you. This emotional rollercoaster usually comprises anxiety, anger and sadness or even depression – not always in that order and sometimes jumbled up together so that it's hard to separate them. Anxiety is about concern for the future or the implications of the change for you or those around you. It's not the same as fear, which is about something real and now, but more about something potential that you anticipate. Our amygdala and hippocampus get locked into a neural loop that seems to feed on itself. There's a lesson here which we return to later on. While fear is an understandable reaction to an imminent threat, with anxiety we effectively do it to ourselves and it may not be helping us. This isn't to judge it unduly – but it does give us some power over it.

Think about our emotions. All an emotion is for is to prompt the body to act in some way – either towards or against something. Once the action is

---

1   Please don't.

2   Both mental and physical illnesses, according to Freud.

performed, the chemicals – the neurotransmitters we met earlier – gradually dissipate. There's no need for them. The result is that emotions (or at least the initial hit) last around 10 to 20 seconds. But, of course, they don't. They linger because of our prefrontal cortex, and we think about them and the causal event, which generates the neurotransmitter hit all over again.

Animals feel emotions (fear, for example) and behave accordingly, but the resulting fight/flight response eventually dissipates the chemicals and normal mood state is resumed.[3] Animals don't spend time afterwards saying to themselves 'Well, *really*. That just wasn't on'. They don't really have much of a sense of future, either, so anxiety isn't generally on their agenda.

But we do, and it is. So we repeat the pattern of thinking and keep on generating the chemical hit, time and time again. We may find ourselves getting angry at the circumstances, other people related or even completely unrelated to the stressful event, or ourselves. As we said before, logic and rationality is not our default during times of change. We may express our anger outwardly or hold it inside, festering away.

depression

Eventually, reality sinks in and with it the (perceived) enormity of the event – and this is where the low point occurs. We all feel sad from time to time, but this process can also lead in some circumstances to outright depression. Martin Seligman suggests that one of the major causes of depression is *learned helplessness* – where we feel out of control of a situation and that the world is happening to us, instead of us happening to the world. If that's how we feel as a result of the change, it's easy to see how this can have an impact. Again, the more control we have, the easier it is to deal with it.

acceptance

Gradually, however, we do usually deal with it. We accept it. It doesn't mean we have to like it or even agree with it, but we put it more into its correct perspective and achieve some sort of proportionality. This is where we start to make choices and start looking to the future. Our frontal lobes gain mastery and we start to plan, make decisions and regain control of our mood state.

an example: redundancy

Let's have a look at this process using the hypothetical example of a redundancy.[4]

---

3   Which is why exercise or going for a long walk or run can temporarily help our mood state.

4   Not autobiographical at all. No, really. Not at all. Nada.

There you are, doing a good job and being generally successful in what you're meant to achieve, when the recession happens and you're called in to the HR Director's office and told that your post is being deleted in a few months. The second part of the conversation becomes a blur: your limbic system is in overload, your heart rate rises temporarily and you find you're unable to concentrate on the conversation. The sabre-toothed cat of redundancy has entered the cave of employment and your amygdala is trying to work out how to respond.

To protect you, your mood state is flattened, and after the initial shock there's a strange sensation of numbness, where you not only don't know how to feel, but you don't know what you're feeling. Eventually, however, after a few days you go into denial, by either putting it to one side and not thinking about it at all or convincing yourself that there must be some mistake – or that they'll change their minds.

Reality then sets in. Anxiety and concern about the future (How am I going to pay the mortgage? What if I never get another job? Who will feed the badger?) is usually first followed by anger and frustration at others (How *dare* they? Don't they realise what they're doing?) and ourselves (I should have spotted it. Why didn't I do something differently?). This goes round and round in your head until the result is a lowered mood state of sadness, or even temporary depression.

Eventually, however, you realise that you're starting to deal with it. You start to understand what parts of this scenario you can control and what you can't, and what choices you have – and what the possible consequences of those choices may be. You start to make plans, make decisions and your old energy returns. You may not be happy at the situation, you may still wish it hadn't happened, and you may think the decision was a flawed one, but the point is you're now dealing with it and accepting it. And moving on. In the end, you may even get to full acceptance or closure on the situation and realise that there were in the end many positives you can take from the situation.

on death and dying

You've probably already seen the link between change (such as redundancy, as in this example) and the process of bereavement. Elizabeth Kübler-Ross pretty much invented this model (in 1969) as a way of describing impending loss and grief, and it's now a recognised way of understanding our reactions to many forms of loss. Although she labels the parts of the curve slightly differently (denial, blaming others, blaming self and confusion leading to eventual acceptance), the process is pretty much the same.

It's been argued that whole organisations can go through this process, as well as the individuals within it. You often hear these sorts of comments at work:

- **Denial**: 'I've seen it all before' or 'If I just keep my head down, it'll pass'.
- **Blaming others**: 'It's the system' or 'The bosses are making us do it'.
- **Blaming self**: 'I can't do it' or 'I'm too old to change'.
- **Confusion**: 'I don't know what to do' or 'Should I stay or should I go?'
- **Acceptance**: 'OK, how do we make this work?' or 'What choices do we now have?'

It's fairly easy to come up with a list of similar phrases about the loss of a loved one. There's a single, rather profound conclusion. Your brain, at a fundamental level, doesn't really distinguish between a change – such as redundancy or an enforced office move – and bereavement. To your limbic system, change is loss.

positive change

It's very easy to fall into the trap of thinking that all the above explanations of how and why change affects us in this way applies only to bad news. After all, it's only logical. But there's the problem. Your limbic system is not too concerned with logic – it has an emotion caused by a neurotransmitter in response to a stimuli, then it just does its thing.

Of course, it's unlikely that if you win £10,000 on the lottery you go through the bereavement cycle, but what if you win £10 million? The history of the lottery is full of examples of people who are unable to cope with the change that large amounts of money makes to their lives. And in a way, something has died: their old self. With this comes a loss of self-identity, their old reasons for working at what they did, a potential loss of friends and their sense of place in the world. There's no point in saying 'Well, what did you do the lottery for?' or 'Why don't you just give it away if it doesn't make you happy?', because that's applying logic when pure logic doesn't always compute during this process.

Positive change can, therefore, have the same impact. When you get married, there's the loss of your old single self;[5] when you move to that house you want, there's the loss of the old; when you get a promotion there's the loss of comfort and your old job description – doing what brought you success in the first place. And if we don't get this bit sorted out, we end up with the Peter

---

5   And certainly the loss of speakers, now relegated behind the sofa.

Principle: being promoted to our level of incompetence because the job's changed and we haven't changed with it.

The point is that this sense of loss often catches us unawares because it's not logical and we didn't expect it. But it can happen anyway. Even if we get what we want.

individual differences

Finally, let's look at why people, notwithstanding the above, vary in their ability to deal with change. The following list isn't exhaustive but gives the general picture. The mere fact that there are so many reasons why our resilience in dealing with change varies means that there's more scope and options to take control of it.

- **Age.** Let's get this one out of the way first. As many of us get older, we get a bit fonder of security and routine, but this is by no means universal. Conversely, many people through maturity and wisdom have more resources and strategies for dealing with change. So, it may have an impact at an individual level, but it's the height of laziness to say that older people can't cope with change. They may also have increased economic security and therefore be better able to get a sense of perspective and proportionality.

- **Differing levels of emotional intelligence.** We explore this in some depth later in the next section as it forms the bedrock of our model for increasing resilience, but for now, the more emotional intelligence we have, the better we're able to deal constructively with change.

- **Personality.** If we take the Myers Briggs Type Indicator (MBTI©) model, for example, as one way of understanding personality variables, then it could be argued that those with a Perceiving preference as opposed to a Judging preference deal more easily with change. Those with a Perceiving preference favour adaptability and flexibility, keeping their options open until the last minute; those with a Judging preference prefer and value closure, completeness, structure and control. Ultimately, of course, this may just reflect the way in which change is dealt with rather than ability to cope with it.[6] We look in more depth at this model in Section 3.

---

6   As a Judging preference person myself, I'm quite happy dealing with change as long as I can control it, or at least put some sort of structure to it. Not everyone likes this model of personality, with some justification, so we'll explore some others later.

- **Attitude**. Again, we explore this in some depth later. We can choose our attitude, and our process for developing resilience through change looks at precisely that. Our attitudes leak into our thoughts and feelings and, therefore, our behaviour.

- **Past experiences**. What doesn't kill you makes you stronger. The more often we go through change and life's experiences, the more often we've built strategies to cope with them. This does depend on attitude, of course – we could also decide we've had enough. The point is, it's a choice.

- **Whatever else is going on**. We have lots of stuff going on at any one time – home, work, finances, health – and going through a work-based change may be the straw that breaks the camel's back. We may be at different points on many different change curves simultaneously.

- **Our genes**. Our genes may influence how sensitive we are to emotional information; those with a variation in a gene[7] that influences the neurotransmitter norepinephrine may pay greater attention to negative words and see the negative aspects of the world more clearly. Not a huge amount you can do about this one, to be fair.

---

7   ADRA2b, if you're interested.

section 2 summary:
how (and why) we react to change

The aim of this section is to give an overview of why we react to change in the way that we do, and what this typically looks like. There are, of course, many variations and variables, but there does seem to be a commonality of experience for most people.

The classic sequence is:

SHOCK » DENIAL » ANXIETY » ANGER » DEPRESSION » ACCEPTANCE

This appears to be common to a range of circumstances, but all seem to have their root in one word: *loss*. Often, this is regardless of logic or proportionality, or how concrete or indeed tenuous the 'loss' is. Just knowing that this is normal and perhaps to be expected can help us be forewarned, and help us make sense of what may appear to be rather irrational thoughts, feelings and behaviours.

key learning points

1. The way we react to change is a function of our evolutionary history as it helped us to survive when under threat.

2. The result is a quick response to threats but it can be rather indiscriminate, as logic isn't involved at this point.

3. The three-part structure of the brain reflects this process: consciously or even unconsciously notice change (threat), pass the input to memory, and feel emotion to enable neurotransmitters to cause our fight or flight behavioural response.

4. We can also route this process through the logical, decision-making part of the brain. This usually happens afterwards, however – and not always then.

5. We learn anything – including our responses to threat and related emotions – by getting neurons to fire (and therefore wire) together. Repeating this firing hardwires the process until it becomes an automated response.

6. The result of this biological and neurological process is the change curve – our classic reactions to change or a stressful event.

7. This is typically Shock » Denial » Anxiety » Anger » Depression » Acceptance.

8. It's exactly the same process as grieving and bereavement, because to your brain that's exactly what change is. A loss of some description.

9. This can even be the case when the change, on the face of it, is positive.

10. There are a variety of factors that mean we all react differently to change, even if the above process remains true for most of us. Age, emotional intelligence, past experiences, personality variables, our attitudes and belief systems, our genetic makeup and any other things simultaneously happening in our lives, all may have an impact on how we respond to a particular event.

exercises

1. Think about a time when you went through a big change. What emotional reactions can you recall? Was there a sequence to them? How long before you got to acceptance? How did these emotional reactions affect your behaviour? What was the impact of your behaviour?

2. Do the same but with a change that – on the face of it, at least – was positive. Do you recognise any of the same reactions?

3. Reflecting on both of these scenarios, what helped you get closure? What were your coping mechanisms or strategies? Who helped you? How long did it take? What do you tell yourself about the changes now?

change and you:
self-awareness

'This above all – to thine own self be true'
William Shakespeare, *Hamlet*

chapter 5

the underpinning concept: emotional intelligence

the journey so far

So. Let's take stock of where we are. We started our journey looking at the wider context of change: why it appears to be inevitable, how it's probably going to happen anyway (with or without us) and the many factors that lead to this.

We then went on to look at why most of us find this uncomfortable at best, debilitating at worse: our brains, using the emotional part rather than the logical part, treat the change as a threat or even akin to bereavement. It often doesn't really matter what the change is about. It could be as important and impactful as redundancy, or as seemingly trivial as giving up your fixed desk to begin hot-desking. To your brain, it doesn't seem to matter. This helped us historically deal with threat by putting us on our guard, of course, but the emotional parts of our brains don't always seem that good at recognising proportionality.

Obviously, however, it's not all hopeless. We deal with it.[1] Most of the time. We usually survive. Some of us are really good and adept at it. And others aren't.

---

1   For any given definition of 'deal' ...

Which means that:

- There are obviously individual differences as to how we deal with change.
- Crashing and burning is not therefore inevitable.

Ergo:

- We must have some control over it. Or more accurately, us.[2]

This, then, is the focus of the rest of this book. If change is inevitable and going to happen anyway, what can we do about it? What's the bit within our control?

Our starting point for understanding this is the concept of *emotional intelligence*, for the simple reason that handling our emotions intelligently is how we successfully deal with change and increase our resilience.[3] In other words, we can learn to recognise and have more control in overriding our initial emotional reactions to change and life's other challenges to enable – or empower – us to behave in ways that help, not hinder us. Which may be the opposite of what we actually want to do at the time.

Therein lies the paradox – and the challenge. We can only control what we're aware of, so increasing our awareness increases the potential for control.

it started with a marshmallow

Or more accurately, two. Imagine being four years old. You're offered a treat such as a marshmallow, which is yours to eat if you want it now. However, if you can wait for 15 minutes, in a room relatively free from distractions, you can have a second.

In a landmark series of studies between 1968 and 1974, the Stanford University psychologist Walter Mischel did just this. What he found was perhaps not surprising: some of the 550 children could do it (typically about a third of them) and some couldn't or decided not to. What's perhaps more interesting is that Mischel followed these children as they grew up, initially over the next 18 years and then again when they were in their 50s, and found the ability to wait for the second marshmallow correlated strongly with later life success: their SATs scores (which had a higher correlation than with their intelligence),

---

2   And as we look at later, this distinction is important.

3   We looked at emotional intelligence, albeit briefly, in *The Psychological Manager: Improve Your Performance Conversations*. The rationale then was that it's primarily the areas covered by the theory of emotional intelligence that make you a great manager of people. Here, we're saying that these areas also make you a great manager of yourself.

popularity, good health and higher incomes. He called this concept the ability to delay gratification: the ability to say no to yourself.[4]

impulse control

This ability to say no to yourself is a key life skill: it determines whether you're likely to revise for exams, work hard to get a promotion and – perhaps even more controversially – whether you demonstrate behaviours that are likely to lead to criminal prosecutions (save up rather than steal, for example). And it's all starting to emerge at the age of four.[5]

Of course, we can now do what Mischel couldn't in the 1970s, and look at what's actually going on in the brain through brain scans. Those with more ability to delay gratification had more activity in (you probably guessed it from Section 2) their prefrontal cortex – the area used for problem-solving, creative and critical thinking, and impulse control.

This body of research was one of Daniel Goleman's starting points for his exploration of emotional intelligence. It's the part concerned with impulse control – for going against our urges when it's more appropriate not to do so. When we have the overwhelming desire to act, especially under times of threat or stress, those of us who're able to ask ourselves 'What's the best way to act in this situation to lead to a successful outcome?' are those who are more successful in dealing with life's challenges. He calls this the master aptitude:

> There is perhaps no psychological skill more fundamental than resisting impulse.
> It is the root of all emotional self-control since all emotions, by their very nature,
> lead to one or another impulse to act.

Although it isn't his concept, no-one has done more to popularise the body of work in this area than Daniel Goleman. A psychologist and *New York Times* journalist, he's the author of several books on emotional intelligence,

---

4   This concept is now taught in many schools as emotional literacy; it seems that four years old is when this ability starts to show – or not. Interestingly, the children used, intuitively, some of the techniques we discuss in Section 4 on mindset mastery. By reframing the marshmallow into a fluffy cloud in their head, or putting an imaginary picture frame around it, they were able to 'cool down' the urge.

5   Or not, as the case may be. It's mainly down to a little bit of genetics and an awful lot of the right kind of parenting. Not over-controlling, as the child won't learn self-control for themselves, and not under-controlling – and also in ensuring children see the consequences of actions. Consistency is the key concept here. It's the child's job to push the boundaries, and the parents' to set them and stick to them. It's this that switches the genes on.

co-authored a psychometric test of it and, perhaps most lucratively, applied the concept to leadership. We return to the link with leadership in Section 5.

back to the brain science

So, first of all, let's relate this to our brain science discussion earlier. Essentially, the literature on emotional intelligence, change and bereavement, and resilience all allude to the same key structures and processes when it comes to our brains. Remember the three-part structure of the brain – the hindbrain, the limbic system and the neocortex (or rational part) – and the way it works together to react in the immediate term to threat. This works because it's quick (no lengthy rational analysis needed to avoid the speeding truck or runaway badger) and it keeps us alive.

But, as we mentioned, our amygdala (where we store or how we catalogue and access emotional memory for instant access) can stick its oar in inappropriately and lead to emotional outbursts or reactions when they're not needed, or even contrary to our best interests. If we know what's stored by our amygdalas (in other words, what winds us up, what specific triggers we can identify and if we can notice the signs when this is all about to kick off) then we're better able to override the process.

The sports psychologist and therapist Steve Peters calls this process the Chimp Paradox. We can think of our limbic system (including the amygdala) as our inner Chimp: faster, stronger and more self-interested than our neocortex (our 'Human'), and usually the first to react. The paradox is that the Chimp is us, but often behaves, well, like a chimp. Chimps are motivated by survival, status and territory. Our inner Chimp craves expression. It's the Human's job to say 'Not now' or 'It's better if we do it this way'. The better able we are to keep our Chimp in the box, the more likely the outcome in non-emergency situations is to work to our advantage.

We return to matters chimp later. For now, the point is that the ability to resist the impulse of our limbic system and behave intelligently with our emotions – not denying or repressing them, but knowing what they are, why they're there in the first place and how to get them under control in the immediate term (and healthily express them in the medium term) – predicts life success. Those who can do this are more resilient in times of change. They're also happier and feel more in control of their lives.

The good news is that we can all get better at it.

why should we?

The short answer is that we just should. The slightly longer answer is that our intellectual intelligence – as measured by IQ tests – is useful to a point. Once we get to a baseline level of intelligence, being brighter doesn't really have much of an impact on job performance, resilience or happiness. Jobs and situations where having a stratospheric IQ is really important are few and far between – academia, engineering and writing books are obvious exceptions.[6] The point is, it's the emotional intelligence bit that makes the difference when IQ reaches this baseline level.[7]

Goleman suggests that IQ alone leaves between 75% and 96% of job success unexplained – it does little to determine who succeeds and fails. Sometimes, it's that indefinable 'They just have it' and sometimes it's standout interpersonal skills – but it will always be about internal strength and resilience. It's been argued that emotional intelligence is roughly twice the predictor of intellectual intelligence when it comes to job – and life – success.

The main point here is that top performers have both. If we have poor emotional intelligence, our intellectual intelligence can get hidden. If we can't manage our emotions or those of others, if we're not self-motivated nor have the resilience to push through temporary setbacks,[8] then our cognitive abilities become almost irrelevant. Remember one of the lessons from Section 2; when we're in the grip of emotion, rational thought goes on a mini-break.

emotional intelligence defined

For our purposes, we can collapse the five or so areas typically classified as emotional intelligence constructs into three core areas:

- **Self-awareness**. This is the ability to recognise your own emotions, when they occur and the reasons for them. You recognise the link between these emotions and your subsequent behaviour, and recognise the impact they

---

6   Not all of this may be true.

7   This baseline level for most professional and technical jobs is an IQ of around one standard deviation above the mean. This is the top end of average – around 115 IQ points, or the top 16% intellectually speaking. Everyone reading this probably has it because you're reading this. And you probably jumped through that hoop at job selection. As everyone else around you jumped through the hoop with you, IQ itself offers little competitive advantage. Being even brighter won't help you, which is just as well, as there's not a huge amount you can do about this.

8   Or if every time the red mist comes down, you wake up with the boss lying in a pool of blood.

may have on others. You know your strengths and your weaknesses, your beliefs and attitudes and whether they help or hinder you. If you have a clear idea of who you are, this is your starting point for deciding who you want to be. And if you know you have a weak spot when it comes to marshmallows, you can put strategies in place to help you resist that first one to get the second ...

- **Self-control**. This is our ability to pass the marshmallow test. People with high self-control can rein in their impulses, say 'No' to themselves and delay gratification because it ends up giving them a better outcome. In times of change, our self-control helps us to maintain a positive mindset, remain calm and more focused. We end up being more resilient and self-motivated, able to maintain drive and energy without being prompted or led by others, and to balance short- and long-term goals in the face of rejection or challenge.

- **Social awareness**. If self-awareness and self-control are about understanding and being able to deal with your own emotions to get to a satisfactory outcome, then social awareness is about being able to read and deal appropriately with the emotions of others. It's about being able to demonstrate empathic understanding, to show sensitivity and awareness of others' perspectives and being able to respond appropriately to get the best out of a situation.[9]

The rest of this section focuses on the first component of emotional intelligence – how to increase your self-awareness – while Section 4 focuses on increasing your self-control in times of change or challenge. We apply the third component of social awareness in Section 5, when we deal with taking a team through change as a manager.

Emotional intelligence describes our potential to learn: we can learn to get better in these areas by developing our emotional competence. This is empowering in a way that a focus on pure intellect is not. Although research into neuroplasticity is making us realise that our intellectual capabilities are perhaps not as fixed as we once thought they were, it's emotional competence that seems to make the biggest difference to job and life success.

Let's start, then, by looking at self-awareness: knowing our inner rudders.

---

9   I said in my first book that being nice and fluffy just doesn't cut it. It's not about being a doormat. At times, demonstrating emotional intelligence may involve being (constructively) challenging and even confrontational. This is what coaches do. You can't be a good coach without high levels of, arguably, all three components of emotional intelligence.

chapter 6

self-awareness: our inner rudder

The first step, then, to increasing our resilience in times of change is to increase our self-awareness. In this chapter, we look at the various ways we can do this.[1]

know thyself

There's a reason why every self-development or leadership development programme, coaching intervention or, for that matter, counselling or therapy session, usually starts with a big dose of self-awareness. It's important to know where we are now before we can get to where we want to go. It's important to know what makes us tick, what doesn't, when we're at our best and when we're not, and what our default styles are. Because knowledge is power.

John Whitmore in his excellent book on coaching[2] puts it succinctly:

I am able to control only that of which I am aware. That of which I am unaware controls me. Awareness empowers me.

---

1   For those of a nervous disposition, here's a warning: I'm going, at some point, to talk about mindfulness.

2   (2009) *Coaching for Performance* (4th edition) London: Nicholas Brealey Publishing.

He actually goes further in suggesting that the whole purpose of coaching is to develop awareness (of ourselves and the situation) and responsibility (truly accepting responsibility for our own thoughts and actions). This is pretty much the focus of this section, because awareness and responsibility lead to choice – and this is where our journey is heading. Everything, ultimately, is a choice. It's all we are. Seven billion choice-machines.

But that's not often how it feels. And the path ahead is often unclear.[3] Sometimes we do have to rely on our gut feelings. Let's just go back to our brain conversation in Section 2. We talked about the hindbrain letting things through to the limbic system, acting as some sort of filter to tell the rest of the brain what to look out for. Although this is true, your brain (through all your senses) notices a lot more than what actually arrives at conscious awareness. It's protecting us from sensory overload, essentially. But it's still there. We just may not realise we know it.[4]

So when we listen to our gut feelings, often we're just tapping into information that we have, but that isn't normally available to us. This could be about the suppressing of emotions, or about more factual information: the point is, our brains take it in, but we don't.

cognitive dissonance

Many of us have had times when we've suppressed uncomfortable feelings about, say, a job or a decision or a relationship, only to realise later on that we should have listened to them – or at least brought them into consciousness to explore them a little further.

As we've said, we can think of consciousness as some sort of control tower, pulling together all the information around us, somewhat independently of thinking about it. If the results seem to be contrary to our actual behaviour we get that nagging or uncomfortable feeling at the back of our mind. Psychologists call this *cognitive dissonance* – and it's your brain's way of saying 'Really? Are you *sure*?' The more self-aware we are (of our thought processes, attitudes, strengths, beliefs and feelings) then the more we have control over them and the more able we are to listen to this inner rudder.

Ultimately, any decision is an emotional one. Logic and rational thought result in lists of alternatives: pros and cons. To decide between them is to

---

3 And full of brambles that rip your shins. Sort of thing.

4 It may trigger emotional memories stored by our amygdalas, for example, which may be important but are encoded.

engage feeling. Most of us get better with age and experience at listening to this emotional steering – we usually call it maturity or wisdom.

As is often the case, science has learned about processes like this by analysing when things go wrong. There are numerous accounts of surgical mistakes which have resulted in the severing of the circuits from the amygdala to the prefrontal lobes, for example. The results are often unimpaired cognitive functioning: the individuals are still able to draw up lists of alternatives with pros and cons of each alternative, they just can't engage their feelings to choose between them. Our limbic system somehow evaluates the data based on prior experience and any other data from our senses that we may not be aware of, and provides us with gut feeling.

So, an intuitive decision is really no such thing. It's a subconscious marrying of logic, experience and emotional impulses that we ignore at our peril. This is not to say it's always right, but we do need to listen to it – and to listen to it means we need to know it's there. We're all capable of burying it away in a box labelled *irrational*.

so, self-awareness is …

Self-awareness, then, is about knowing your emotions: what you're feeling, when and why, and how these link with your behaviour. Behaviour includes your actions, your happiness, your resilience and your work performance.

It's about knowing your strengths, weaknesses, preferences, attitudes and belief systems and biases (more on all these later) and therefore being able to question them. The result is an inner confidence, being able to make decisions more quickly and using your inner values to decide what the right course of action is.

This is why organisations sometimes develop and publish a set of Values – they enable an employee, when unsure of how to act in a particular scenario, a type of shortcut to guide them to make a decision according to overarching principles. If you then decide you don't agree with those principles, you can choose to leave and work somewhere else where the Values fit.

raising awareness

You'll realise by now that raising our levels of awareness is a Good Thing. There are, of course, many ways to do this. Let's look at a few of the simple and more obvious ones first:

- Get more feedback.
- Go through Appraisal data.
- Self-reflection.
- Coaching, counselling and therapy.
- Mindfulness.

First of all, getting more feedback.

feedback

It's interesting how we often have an emotional reaction to the thought of getting feedback. In my experience, when people say 'I love feedback, bring it on', what they usually mean is 'Tell me how great I am'. We often treat more negative feedback (and feedback is usually both positive *and* negative) as a threat, which, of course, gets our limbic system twitching.

David Rock[5] identifies five threats that really get our amygdalas flashing, which he calls the SCARF model, and many of them can be affected by receiving feedback. Don't forget that our brain, in trying to protect us, is essentially moving away from pain and towards pleasure, so any perceived threat gets it agitated. As we mention these five areas, think how they may apply to receiving feedback and you'll see what we're up against.

status

We spend a lot of our internal energy defending our sense of status. This appears to be tapping into ancient survival drives: higher status animals tend to live longest in the group. When we perceive ourselves (or get feedback to suggest it) as higher status than others, it feels good. We get a little hit of the neurotransmitter dopamine and this, in theory at least, reinforces the behaviour that made us appear high status, so we do it more. So we survive.

Of course, the opposite is also true. If we receive feedback that knocks that sense of status, we get hit with lowered dopamine levels, and we even generate the more stressy chemicals, such as cortisol. We can do this to ourselves as well, of course. If we constantly compare ourselves adversely to other people, then that becomes a threat to our inner sense of status. We don't always need

---

5   (2009) *Your Brain at Work*. New York: HarperCollins.

someone else to do it for us.

In any event, we have a deep-rooted motivation to preserve our sense of status. The brain's innate tendency to exaggerate threat and focus on the negative doesn't help! The message here, then, is not only be careful how you give feedback, but also be careful how you ask for it and how you take it. Perceived loss of status is regarded by the brain as a threat. Appendix 3 gives an example of how to ask for feedback constructively, but do remember perspective: use it or lose it.

certainty

Our brains crave it. It generates dopamine again. We like to see patterns that we can quickly make sense of, and when we can't, the resulting uncertainty is uncomfortable – even leading to the stress response. During times of change, of course, we may be even more tuned in to expecting uncertainty, which is going to put us on edge.

In terms of relating to feedback, this depends on how accurate our self-assessment of whatever we get feedback on, actually is. If we have an over-inflated sense of how good we are at something, and then receive feedback that's less than complimentary, then our sense of certainty is inevitably knocked.

autonomy

One of themes of this book is about recognising that most of what we think, feel and do is a choice. It doesn't always feel it, but there you go. Autonomy is about the power and freedom to make choices, and if this power or freedom is curtailed, then we meet our old friend stress. There's a wealth of research which demonstrates that people with more autonomy over their lives live longer (presumably due in part to the detrimental effects of living with stress among those with poor autonomy).

Although this one may not have much impact on getting feedback per se (although you could argue that having more knowledge leads to identifying more choices), it certainly has an impact in the wider context of change, so we'll return to this point later.

relatedness

This was discussed in some depth in my first book, when looking at group identity. Our sense of who we are and our value to society is inextricably linked to the groups to which we belong. It's an essential part of the human condition and obviously has its roots in survival back in our distant hunter-gatherer past. Neurologically, we're wired to tune in to others' emotions and feel the same thing: emotions are contagious because there was an evolutionary advantage to them being so. We have to be careful when we're the boss – the boss's emotions tend to be picked up more powerfully by others.[6]

Anyway, this basic *in-group/out-group* psychology drives a lot of our feelings and behaviour, and so receiving feedback on our team orientation and place in the group may have a profound impact, depending on the nature of that feedback. Feeling part of a group we value generates the 'You are my friend' chemical, oxytocin, which feels nice. So we try to do more of it. If we receive feedback that we could be more of a team player, for most of us it's not going to feel good.

fairness

This one is perhaps more obvious to understand in a 'receiving feedback' sense. If we receive feedback that we perceive as unfair (or if it's given in an unconstructive, clumsy or harsh way) then our threat response is likely to be generated. If feedback is given in this way it actually becomes a pointless exercise, as our brains prepare for fight or flight and – as we've seen – logic, rationality and information-processing take a back seat.

useful feedback

So, that's the SCARF model. As for what we want to receive feedback on, this obviously depends on what awareness we want to generate. There's nothing wrong with fairly generic 'What do I do well and what can I do better?' requests, but make sure to get examples of behaviours rather than vague generalisations. Some example questions are detailed in Appendix 3.

Receiving 360 degree feedback takes this to a new level. Usually automated and often built around an organisation's competency framework, the process usually asks respondents to rate the individual on a set of specific questions on a numeric scale. An example might be 'To what extent does X regularly request feedback about their performance?', with the choices being from 1 (never) to 5 (very often). These questions are then collapsed into competency order so an individual can see how they're doing in the perceptions of others in discrete behavioural areas *that the organisation values*. Useful information.

Usually, the individual chooses who will respond in specific categories (manager, direct reports, peers, customers, etc) and the individual also

---

6 If you want to know what sort of a day you're going to have, look at the boss's mood at 9am ...

completes the same questionnaire on themselves. Looking at any differences in scores between self and others, or between groups, is useful data that you can do something with. These 360 degree questionnaires often have an additional 'What does X do well?' and 'What could X do differently?' free-text sections at the end to add more flavour – this is usually the bit that generates the SCARF domain threats mentioned above!

The point about feedback is that knowledge is power, and it's useful to see how others view you. The trick is to remember that it's always about perception: perception is not necessarily reality, but we can still do something with the information. Feedback is often contradictory – it then means you have to think about whether you behave differently in different scenarios or with different people.

Think in advance about the areas you particularly want to receive feedback on – the more specific you can be, the more specific (and therefore useful) the responses will be. And if you receive less than complimentary feedback, the techniques we look at later will help you to get a sense of perspective. Try not to get defensive or immediately try to justify your behaviour or performance. It doesn't help and is likely to be amygdala-led. After all, it's just data, essentially. And it may or may not be true.

appraisal data

You can also go back through your appraisal data over the last few years.[7] Its usefulness will obviously depend on the rigour with which your organisation or manager(s) undertook the exercise, but it can all add to the mix.

Think about the themes that have emerged over several years if you can, and ask yourself the following questions:[8]

- What strengths have emerged over the years?
- How (and in what) have I grown?
- What have I particularly enjoyed over the years?
- When was I at my best?
- What developmental themes keep occurring?
- What have I done about them?
- What challenges have I overcome?

---

7   If your experience is anything like mine, this may be rather, erm, vague.

8   See Appendix 4.

- What qualities did I use to overcome them?
- What do I want next year's appraisal to say?
- What can I start doing now to make this more likely?

Obviously, this exercise is more useful for some than others, depending on your particular organisation or manager. Even if you haven't had formal appraisals over the last few years,[9] it's still a useful thought-exercise to go through on your own. Which leads us on to self-reflection as an exercise.

self-reflection

I spend quite a lot of my time helping teams to identify the *processes* of their working together, as opposed to merely the *content*, or what they work on. Indeed, one of the parameters of being a High Performing Team suggests just that – they periodically spend time out to look at the way the team is working. They look at what's going well and what needs to be changed, what communication is like, how decisions are made, problems solved and how conflict is dealt with. They identify the team's collective strengths and how they can be used synergistically so the team is more than the sum of its parts. They also look at what successes they've had and what can be built on – and where they need to be in, say, a year's time.

A really useful exercise, I'm sure you agree. How often, then, do we take time out to do this for ourselves – our work, our career aspirations, our happiness? I'm as guilty as anyone in not doing this, despite quoting the Socratic (or possibly Platonic) 'An unexamined life is not worth living' concept at people. It didn't seem to be that important when I had colleagues to discuss these things with and share notes on a more ad hoc basis. Working for myself, it's become essential. I've had to modify my natural tendency towards extraversion, to introspection: to take time to look at what's going on with my business, my development, my aspirations for my future and my job satisfaction – and ultimately my happiness.[10]

Anyway. Enough about me. If you receive coaching support (life, business or career) then one of the activities given for your homework is usually focused

---

9   I've met many people who have never had an appraisal, or – believe it or not – don't actually know who their manager is. And I've met teams who do each other's appraisals because the manager won't.

10 It seems to me that if you don't enjoy it, then you should stop. Whatever it is. There's a 1970s' joke (I think attributed to Tommy Cooper) which goes something like (when raising his arm) 'Doctor, it hurts when I do that', to which the reply is 'Well, don't do it'. We often carry on doing it because we haven't realised that it's *that* which is doing the hurting.

on self-reflection, often in the form of some sort of reflective diary. In much the same way as we identified getting feedback from others, we can (and should) do the same for ourselves – using pretty much the same questions, with the addition of questions on future aspirations which others may not be aware of.

It doesn't matter if you don't know where you want to be in five or ten years' time (although it certainly helps if you can identify where you want to be in, say, a year or so), but the point is to get used to the inner reflection time. Learn what the introvert does (or purposely engage your own inner introvert – we all have one). If we have at least some idea where we want to end up – or whether we want to keep our options as open as possible – then we can start purposely putting things into place to make it more likely to happen.

reflection exercise

You can also use this reflection exercise to look at how to gain awareness of your responses to change or stressful situations. This can help to give you data for the future – and therefore more choices, and more control.

Think about a time when you were under stress or pressure, or about a stressful or challenging time you're facing right now. Ask yourself these questions:[11]

- What's challenging or stressful about it? Why?
- What impact does it have on me emotionally? How do I know?
- How does it make me feel? What emotion could I call it?
- What do I notice physically? When did this start?
- What impact does it have on my colleagues or family?

Write your answers down; we return to them later in a follow-up exercise.

The more we can analyse and interpret what's making us stressed or unhappy, the more we can notice when it starts to happen and put mechanisms in place to deal with it more constructively. It gives you time to make more choices before the limbic system goes into overdrive. This is the essence of the self-control part of emotional intelligence.

coaching

There's also coaching. If you can afford it[12] then coaching is an excellent tool to help generate self-awareness. We explored coaching in some depth in *The*

---

11   A template is in Appendix 5.

12   Or persuade your employer to pay for it ...

*Psychological Manager: Improve Your Performance Conversation*s from a line management perspective – i.e. how to do it – and we can obviously use some of the principles and techniques on ourselves, and self-coach.

Let's take a relevant part of my original introduction to the topic from that first book, as I couldn't put it better myself for a second time. You'll remember from above that the essence of coaching is raising awareness and responsibility:

> *By building awareness, we give our coachee some control back; we can't control what we're not aware of. Through focused attention, questioning and reflecting we can help our coachee be more tuned in to the essence of their problem – and potential solutions. By building responsibility, we're making it clear that the answer to their problem lies within them and that the choices they make are theirs, no-one else's. When we tell someone what to do, or even give our best-intentioned advice, we unwittingly take on some of that responsibility without the power to do anything with it.*[13]

Whether we attempt to self-coach using the techniques outlined in my first book or we get a coach, the point is that we can improve our self-awareness using this basic philosophy: we know the answers that are right for us but may need a tool to get them out.

One more paragraph from last time as to why it works:

> *Being coached gives us our calm space. It can help us reduce the emotional arousal we experience about events, or threats to our status or independence, and allows us to start engaging the thinking parts of our brain. Somewhat ironically, the act of problem-solving with someone else can also stop us from overthinking a problem, and allow us to express the more subtle insights we may have. And as our coach is a step removed from the issue, their insights may also be tentatively added to the mix.*

Anyway. Appendix 6 may help.

Taking this up a gear, we could also gain insight by having counselling or therapy. Not something to go into lightly, to be honest, and in this country at least it doesn't yet appear to be the norm as an exercise for gaining self-awareness; it's more often than not used to help someone deal with something specific that's troubling them or that they're struggling to cope with (or are learning to become a counsellor or therapist themselves). It's mentioned here more for the sake of completeness, but of course is a perfectly valid option.

---

13   See Appendix 4.

mindfulness

Here's another one we can do ourselves. Mindfulness practice.[14] An awful lot has been written about mindfulness over the last couple of years and it still seems to be gaining momentum. It is, in effect, meditation without any religious connotations, and as such is suitable for religious and non-religious people equally. You don't even have to set aside time to do it (but it's best if you do to start with) as you can use the technique during any activity – particularly that long commute.[15]

The principle is easy, the practice less so – but gets better with time. It's essentially being completely and wholly immersed in a moment or activity by noticing what's around you – sights, sounds, smells, etc – and focusing on (and only on) them. The point is to just accept what is there; notice interrupting thoughts and let them go.

So. What's the point? The idea is that if we can periodically quieten our minds and focus purely on the here and now (by, say, focusing on our breathing), then it gives our nervous system time to recover and sharpen. It eventually helps us to increase self-awareness by being able to notice very early on when we're having unhelpful or negative thoughts (that inevitably lead to negative emotions[16] and possibly stress). We're then empowered to accept them for what they are, then move on by allowing them to drift away. They are just thoughts and feelings, but they are not *you*. As I say, easy in principle ...[17]

There's actually evidence that mindfulness can work. Several studies have found that repeated practice can result in lowered stress and worry, and can lead to an increased sense of wellbeing and perceived health.[18] Research shows that it can lead to better emotional regulation and actually change brain structures[19] as measured by neuroimaging techniques. It's increasingly being used in clinical psychology and psychiatric settings as well as schools, prisons and hospitals. The NHS website has some guidance.[20]

---

14 I warned you.

15 Not if you're driving, obviously.

16 Like wet paint attracts suicidal flies. (There may be a better analogy.)

17 There are apps that can take you through guided mindfulness sessions. Check out *Headspace*, for example.

18 Branstrom, R., Duncan, L.G. & Moskowitz, J.T. (2011). 'The association between dispositional mindfulness, psychological well-being, and perceived health in a Swedish population-based sample', *Br J Health Psychol* 16 (2): 300–16; Baer, R.A., Smith, G.T., Lykins, E. et al (2008). 'Construct validity of the five facet mindfulness questionnaire in meditating and nonmeditating samples', *Assessment* 15 (3): 329–42.

19 The anterior cingulate cortex and temporo-parietal junction, apparently. If you're interested.

20 www.nhs.uk

The technique is virtually indistinguishable from meditation. There's an example of a guided practice session in Appendix 7. Start small – say in 10-minute blocks – and gradually increase the time if you find it useful.[21] In the end, you can practise it while commuting, going for a walk, eating a raisin or washing up. Research shows that a short course in mindfulness leads to brain changes similar in nature to those seen in people who have practised spiritual meditation for a lifetime.[22]

Mindfulness, then, can help us prevent the tunnel vision that we often drift into when looking at our immediate world. We become more aware of the present moment and understand ourselves better – we can make sense of the stream of consciousness going on in our heads at any one time and therefore take more control of it, or notice patterns that either help or hinder us.

So. We've looked at some simple techniques for raising awareness. Chapters 7–9 look at some more in-depth ones: understanding your motivational drivers, your personality and your strengths.

---

21   To be honest, gradually increase the time if you don't, as well. It may well become useful the longer you do it.
22   A systematic review published in *Brain and Cognition* and reported in *The Psychologist*, Vol. 29, No. 12.

chapter 7

self-awareness: motivational drivers

In this and subsequent chapters, we spend some time examining the key drivers behind your behaviour, using three concepts:[1]

- Motivation
- Personality
- Strengths.

The idea is that knowing your key drivers and preferences in these three areas helps you gain awareness of when you're at your best. It also increases your awareness of others' drivers. We are all different and have different motivational needs, personality preferences and work-based strengths, and

---

1   I've covered these three areas before: the first two in *The Psychological Manager: Improve Your Performance Conversations* (from a managerial perspective) and the third in my second book *Get that Job in 7 Simple Steps,* which looked at Strengths from a career coaching perspective. Although we're putting a different spin on these concepts, the principles are the same – but it's useful having them all in one place. (Buy the other books as well, though.)

knowing how people differ in these areas (and that it's not only OK but usually and – in a team, at least – helpful) helps us to understand who we are.

motivation

In *The Psychological Manager: Improve Your Performance Conversations* we spent some time talking about motivation from the perspective of line management; we took an in-depth journey through motivation research and theory over the last 100 years, and where we are now. I'm not going to repeat this here, so here's a summary:

- Based on old military models of leadership, early research was behaviourist in approach: people need coercing through wage incentive schemes, other carrots or, indeed, sticks. Taylor's Scientific Management school, based on his work on 1920s' Ford production lines, treated workers as cogs in wheels, out for what they could get – if you change the stimulus, you get a different response.[2] This was all part of the behaviourist drive to make psychology a real science after all that Freudian mumbo-jumbo.

- Later, the humanists (and to some extent the cognitive scientists) complained that the point is that we are all individual and have individual (albeit predictable) needs and drivers. In other words, we typically go through a hierarchy of needs, with one level of need having to be satisfied before we can concentrate or be motivated by the next level. The mechanism by which this happens is our old friend, cognitive dissonance, who we met earlier, and it was Maslow who conceptualised this model as a hierarchy.

- Herzberg took this model and suggested that factors outside the job itself (like pay, benefits, terms and conditions and the environment in which we work) have a small and temporary effect on our motivation, and ultimately performance. We need to be paid enough to get the subject off the table (otherwise we're distracted and de-motivated) so we can then focus on higher order, more intrinsic motivators (development, recognition, variety and autonomy, for example) which have a deeper, more sustainable impact on motivation.

I suggested that the end product of all this was to enable line managers to have conversations with their teams to help them identify their key motivational

---

2   Think 'Pavlov' and you won't be far wrong.

drivers, and then to see if the job (elements of a small project or wider job itself) can be tweaked to be more in tune with the individual's personal drivers. I suggested using a list to help prompt the conversation and to get their teams to identify their top three motivational drivers at the moment (although they remain fairly stable,[3] drivers are subject to change as life experiences change), and then see what can be done to tweak the job or add bits to it.

your motivational drivers

The above 100 years of research has pretty much given us a list to choose from, and I use the example list (given here as Appendix 8), which is as good as any. Take a look at this list, and ask yourself the following questions:

- What are the three that most appeal to me?
- What were they five years ago?
- How does my current role reflect these drivers?

We'll come back to these follow-up questions later ...

- What conversations can I have to make sure there's a good match with my job?
- What can I do to ensure there's more of a match?
- What does this say about my future aspirations?

Remember that what we're saying here is that if you can make your job look as much like your key motivational drivers as you can, then that's you on a good day. Bear in mind that the bottom three on the list (Material, Security and Environment) are what Herzberg called Hygiene factors[4] and although they have a temporary impact (and may be temporarily important[5]), the other items on the list have more of an intrinsically motivating effect and are more likely to lead to you on that good day.

---

3 I've always had a strong need for autonomy. Ask my mother.
4 I assume because they're like a good wash. It works for a while but then you have to do it again to get the motivational impact (or cleansing effect). We then get desensitised to it, so come to expect the pay rise and are demotivated if we don't get it.
5 My Security need went through the roof when I was made redundant.

an economist's view

An interesting economist's take on motivation was given recently by Dan Pink.[6] Although he agrees that the Hygiene factors such as pay and benefits are important, we just need to have enough to take the issue off the table. The three most important motivating drives for him (in other words, what seems to have the biggest impact in driving human behaviour economically) are:

- **Autonomy**: the power to make our own decisions and work on what we want. Pink gives the example of a software organisation allowing staff to work on anything they like one day a quarter as long as they show the results – and found that it was the most usefully (organisationally) productive day by far.
- **Mastery**: the inherent desire most of us have just to get better at something. When we feel we're progressing at something, we get a little satisfying hit of dopamine that makes us want to do more of it.
- **Purpose**: most of us want to work on something that's worthwhile, that has a point and may be part of something bigger than ourselves. We crave meaning in our lives and when we find what it is, it creates its own pull.

Have a think about these as well. How are you satisfying these basic needs? It doesn't have to be all about work, of course – I'm spending some of my downtime trying to be less appalling on the piano – so take your life in the round.

Understand what typically motivates you and how you can make your work (and home life) fit these motivational drivers. This is not only an important line management tool: it's an important part of your own self-awareness.

---

6   I show his animated video clip *Drive* in my training.

8

self-awareness: personality

We covered the concept of personality before[1] and the interested reader can look there if they want to understand the journey that psychological thought has taken: from Hippocrates' four humours, through Freud's fixation stages and structure of personality (id, ego, super-ego), to more cognitive and humanistic concepts via behaviourism.

Here we're more concerned with the measurement of personality in order to help your own self-awareness.

In *The Psychological Manager: Improve Your Performance Conversations* we called the type of theory that looks at the dimensions of personality – as opposed to how it develops – nomothetic models. Freud et al were looking at where personality comes from, but for our purposes, we just need to understand how it's structured. This aids our awareness of our preferences and styles so we can use them to our advantage during times of change or challenge. This is essentially for the same reason as we undertake 360 degree

---

[1]   Chapter 8 in the award-nominated first book. If I don't say it, no-one else will. I've borrowed some bits here.

feedback processes (described in Chapter 6) when, for example, designing management development programmes: know what your default styles and strengths are and we're better placed to be able to adapt or stretch them.

Various models are used, so let's just explore a few of them so you're aware of how individuals differ and where your preferences might sit.[2] There are two main types: *type* and *trait*.

trait approaches

The nomothetic approach tends to make use of the concept of traits when referring to dimensions of personality. Traits are those aspects of personality that we all have, to a greater or lesser extent. When psychometric tests are designed along the theoretical frameworks laid down by the great trait theorists (Eysenck, Cattell), they're structured so that each trait is normally distributed along the classic bell curve; individuals assessing themselves through these questionnaires are compared to a large sample of people who've taken the test before (a norm group), and so will see where they stand on the normal distribution curve.

An example would be the trait *Dominance*: the right-hand side of the bell curve is the Dominant end and at the left is the Submissive end, with most people being in the middle. Your score determines where on this curve you see yourself compared to the comparison group (usually General Population, UK Managers and Professionals, or Graduates).

A trait, then, is generally thought of as a relatively stable pattern of behaviour or other aspect of personality. Although the principles behind the various trait theorists remain the same, arguably the main contentious issue is the number of traits that adequately describe human behaviour. Hans Eysenck contended that this number could be reduced to three: *Extraversion*, *Neuroticism* and *Psychoticism*. Questionnaires based on Eysenck's work[3] tend to be used more for research purposes than occupational ones, but he does remain one of the most cited theorists in the history of psychology. Eysenck was in almost constant battle with our next trait theorist, Raymond Cattell, over the number of traits that personality can be usefully broken down to, but their similarities vastly outweigh their differences. It just depends on how you cut the personality cake.

---

2   To formally assess these preferences, you may have to enlist the services of a trained consultant. Don't do a freebie on the interweb. They are usually fake and written like horoscopes: 'Under huge amount of pressure, you may find yourself getting rather tense' sort of thing.

3   The Eysenck Personality Inventory (EPI) and Eysenck Personality Questionnaire (EPQ).

Cattell: 16PF

Through his analysis (using everyday life behaviours, data from experimental situations and questionnaire data) Cattell came up with 16 fundamental factors (he called them primary factors) underlying human personality, each with its own associated set of behaviours. These factors remain relatively stable over time, although they can be temporarily affected by mood state.

Cattell named these factors after the letters of the alphabet to avoid any preconceptions associated with existing terms, and developed one of the world's most widely used personality questionnaires – the 16PF™ – to measure them. This questionnaire is used for a variety of purposes: selection, development, coaching and counselling, and in clinical settings.[4]

On the 16PF™, each trait or factor is normally distributed (an individual's score can be mapped on to the bell-shaped curve) with separate descriptions for left-hand and right-hand positions, and with most of the population falling in the middle. Examples are:

- **Factor A:** *Warmth*. The left-hand position refers to a tendency to be reserved, cool and detached, and right-hand positions as outgoing and warmhearted, *compared to the average*.
- **Factor C:** *Emotional Stability*. The left-hand position refers to emotional instability and being easily upset, and the right-hand as more emotionally stable, calm and mature.

An individual's scores on each of the 16 factors can therefore be visually represented as a profile for ease of interpretation. A list of all 16 traits is in Appendix 9. This approach is also used by subsequent questionnaires, such as SHL's Occupational Personality Questionnaire (OPQ32r[5]): again, this is widely used in industry for both selection and development purposes.

When Cattell factor-analysed these 16 factors, he found that they can collapse down to five second-order, or *global*, factors: each one of these five is made up of four or five primary factors that tend to go together in the real world. As an example, an individual's score on the global factor *Extraversion*

---

4   My first proper job as an Occupational Psychologist was with the 16PF™ publishers for the UK version of the questionnaire, and I spent my four years there training people to be qualified to use it. Somewhat coincidentally (I assume) Cattell died on the day I joined.

5   Guess how many traits this one measures …

is made up of their scores on five primary factors: *Warmth, Vigilance, Social Boldness, Privateness* and *Self-reliance*. If each of these scores is high (or low on *Privateness* as the scale is reversed), the result is a high score on *Extraversion*.

the Big Five

These five global factors are important. The vast majority of research and cross-validation with other personality questionnaires suggests that personality has these five over-arching domains, now known in personality theory as the Big Five. This is heartening for the practitioner: we can be pretty confident that we're using a model that's empirically driven from a variety of sources.[6]

These Big Five are known by the acronym OCEAN:

- *Openness*: appreciation for variety, creativity, culture, independence.
- *Conscientiousness*: self-discipline, responsibility, planned rather than spontaneous.
- *Extraversion*: outgoing, energetic, seeks company, sociable.
- *Agreeableness*: good-natured, friendly and compassionate, cooperative.
- *Neuroticism*: sensitive, nervous, experiences strong emotions, less emotionally stable (now often called *Emotional Stability*[7]).

You'll notice that both Cattell's and Eysenck's work is reflected here. As mentioned, the 16PF™ and EPQ measure all or some of the Big Five, the OPQ32r can be used to give an assessment of them and the NEO Personality Inventory measures them specifically.[8]

type approaches

There's one major model here that many people are familiar with: the Myers Briggs Type Indicator (MBTI©). Often used in individual and team development,

---

6   'The "Big Five" has become a widely accepted template for understanding the structure of human personality' (Arnold, J. & Randall, R. et al (2010). *Work Psychology* (5th edition). London: Prentice Hall, p 116).

7   Presumably a rather more PC term.

8   Costa, P.T. & McCrae, R.R. (1985). *The NEO Personality Inventory Manual*. Odessa, FL: Psychological Assessment Resources.

it's currently the world's most used model of individual differences.[9] This is another useful framework to help you understand your team's dynamics, and their typical ways of communicating with each other and the outside world.

the MBTI

This is one of the more useful models of personality in that it's both relatively easy to understand, and has practical implications for the way you manage your team and the individuals within it. A brief overview of the theory and model follows: if you wish to explore this model with your team (and completing/ getting feedback on the Indicator itself often forms part of a team building session), then you'll need the services of a qualified practitioner.

Like all theories of personality, the MBTI© (based primarily on Jungian theory) assumes that the important aspects of our personality are stable (as opposed to fixed) and tend towards consistency over time and situations. Jung discovered through his clinical work that people tend to behave – in certain key areas of psychological functioning – in predictable, consistent ways.

The central concept is one of *preference*: we have a preference for behaving in ways that we're most comfortable with, or in doing what comes naturally. This is not the only way we behave in any situation, but the most common one, and one which is (usually) when we (re)act at our best because we're most used to it. These preferences are not abilities, being more concerned with style or patterns of behaviour rather than the quality of the end result.

All preferences have equal value, and all have their strengths and weaknesses: an analogy with your preference for being left- or right-handed is often used, which can lead to all sorts of interesting discussions about the genetic propensities of Jungian types.

The MBTI© has four bipolar pairs of preferences, and an individual is assumed to prefer behaving according to one of each pair of opposites over the other. This inevitably leads to the 'It depends on the situation' argument – but again, we use our left hand for activities occasionally even if we have a preference for using our right.

---

9   Despite empirical evidence for its reliability and validity being somewhat sketchy. A lot of academics don't like it. In my experience, most of the problems are about it being used badly, for the wrong reasons or about the actual psychometric properties of the questionnaire itself, as opposed to the model per se. In my view, despite these valid concerns, the model is still a useful way of conceptualising personality preferences and individual differences. If you want more on this, see Pittenger, D.J. (2005). 'Cautionary Comments Regarding the Myers Briggs Type Indicator', *Consulting Psychology Journal: Practice and Research*, Vol. 57(3).

This is primarily how a *type* approach to personality differs from a *trait* one. With a trait, it's assumed that we all have a bit of it to a greater or lesser extent (such as *Dominance*); with type, it's an 'either-or' preference, which can result in feeling labelled if used clumsily. It's important to remember that we use all eight options at various times, but we tend to have our defaults when we operate at our best.

These four dichotomies are:

- **E**xtraversion or **I**ntroversion (where we prefer to get and focus our energy).
- **S**ensing or **IN**tuition (the type of information we focus on and trust).
- **T**hinking or **F**eeling (how we process information and make decisions).
- **J**udging or **P**erceiving (how we deal with the world around us).

According to the theory, therefore, an individual's MBTI Type will comprise four letters: one from E/I, S/N, T/F and J/P respectively. The sum is truly greater than the sum of the parts, however: as well as a description for each side of each pairing, there's an overall description for each one of the 16 possible combinations of these four preferences that goes beyond the individual descriptions. A summary of these preferences is given in Appendix 10.

You may want to think through these eight dimensions, making notes of your preferences and examples of when you demonstrated them. Remember – we all do all eight, but you will, on balance, have a preference.

chapter 9

self-awareness: strengths

Let me start with a little story. There was a chap in the late 1960s who liked to electrocute dogs. Well, I say *like*, but he did it anyway. It was OK because he was (is) a psychologist. And he didn't really electrocute them as such, but rather put them in a cage and passed a small(ish) current through the floor.

There was a point to this, by the way. It wasn't just for fun.[1] He put a lever in the cage, and at first, by accident, the dog pressed the lever in its discomfort and the shock stopped. After a few repeats, the dog learned through conditioning (think Pavlov) that the lever stopped the shock. No particular ill-effects on the dog because – and here's the important bit – it had learned that it had control over its environment.

The second part of the experiment involved – you guessed it – disconnecting the lever. The result was very different. With the lever no longer stopping the shocks, the dog eventually just sat in a corner, demonstrating all the symptoms of clinical depression. It often didn't even try to get out of the cage, even when the door was opened.

---

1   Psychologists don't really do anything for fun. Unless you count the lap-dancing research, and that only works for some, I guess.

learned helplessness

The difference is that this time, the dog has learned something else: that it is powerless in its environment – and this led to the dog suffering a depressive illness. The particular psychologist involved was called Martin Seligman, and he called this concept *learned helplessness* – still regarded as one of the causes of depression in humans. When we feel out of control and that the world is happening *to* us, we can get lowered mood states.

Anyway, wind forward 30 years. This same psychologist had started to feel that the profession of psychology tended, reasonably enough, to focus on when things are going wrong: depression, anxiety, personality disorders, psychopathy and countless other psychological disorders of mind and behaviour. He felt that as a discipline, psychology has much to offer in trying to help people who aren't necessarily clinically ill, but want to think and behave at their best. As a result, Seligman – along with others – founded the Positive Psychology movement, and one of its outputs was research into the world of work-based strengths.[2]

And the link with the dogs? If to some extent we can learn that we're helpless, which can cause depression, we can obviously learn to be powerful, optimistic and happy, too. To some degree (it's been mentioned before, and we look at this in subsequent chapters), happiness can be thought of as an attitude – and is therefore a choice.

optimising our strengths: flow

Identifying our key strengths is therefore important. When we perform any task, being aware of our strengths and turning up the dial on them creates us on a good day. If we apply them to achieve something meaningful, something perhaps with a higher purpose (see Dan Pink's Autonomy, Mastery and Purpose model in Chapter 7) then that creates optimal happiness and fulfilment – and, of course, peak performance. Seligman has written extensively about the links between optimising your strengths to achieve meaningful pursuits, psychological and physical health, and even longevity.

---

2   In his TED talk of February 2004 ('The new era of positive psychology') Seligman recounts the tale of being asked by CNN to comment on the state of psychology today in a one-word soundbite. 'Good,' was his reply. In two words? they asked. 'Not good' was his witty rejoinder. In three words? 'Not good enough.' His point was that psychology was good at making people less miserable, but not good enough at helping those of us without such disorders to be any fitter, happier, more productive. His aim and the aims of his colleagues, such as Mihaly Csikszentmihalyi, was to use psychological principles to nurture high talent and help people be, well, happy. Not just not unhappy.

When we feel we're really optimising our strengths on something purposeful, one of the other founding members of the Positive Psychology movement, Mihaly Csikszentmihalyi (we met him briefly in Section 1) called this being in a state of *flow*. In a state of flow time stands still: we're totally absorbed in the moment and are, in a manner of speaking, at one with the music. It isn't that we feel good necessarily – that comes afterwards – but in the flow state itself we don't really feel anything, just total immersion in the task.

When we're in flow, we're usually at the top of our Yerkes-Dodson arousal curve.[3] This is the classic inverted U-shape, where our performance goes up as our arousal and 'stress' goes up until we reach a peak. Further stress and arousal leads to our performance going back down the curve again. We need some stress to perform (through increased levels of noradrenaline, for example) but this needs to be balanced with other chemicals such as dopamine, which makes us feel good. When the two are in balance, we make brain connections more easily and we perform at our best – at the top of the curve. Too much stress means we can't focus – too little means we don't.

All of this requires self-awareness again; knowing what your strengths are and how to use them at their optimum to keep them in that Goldilocks zone – not too little, not too much, but just right. Strengths are not the things you know or the experience you have. Those are your skills. Strengths are those 'underlying qualities that energize us, contribute to our personal growth and lead to peak performance'.[4] Apply your strengths to your skills and you bring your best self to whatever it is you're doing.

our significant seven strengths …

How do we identify our key work-based strengths? The Strengths Partnership have come up with a framework of 24 work-based strengths that extensive research told them had the biggest impact on work performance. A trained consultant[5] can take you through a psychometrically rigorous questionnaire and give you a report. The same, of course, applies to the MBTI© model described in Chapter 8, and I often use the two in tandem when a hefty dose of self-awareness is needed.

---

3   That's one to bring out at parties. On second thoughts, I wonder if that's why I don't get invited to parties.

4   Brewerton & Brook (2006). These are the founding partners of The Strengths Partnership, whose Strengths model I use a great deal – and is the model we use here. Check out www.strengthspartnership.com. They're lovely people and it's a great model.

5   Hello.

Although the questionnaire and report give you an ultimately more rigorous assessment, you can just look at the model itself (Appendix 11) and pick your significant seven strengths from the 24. These are not the strengths you'd like to have or think you should have, but the seven that you feel most describe you. Have a go now.

It will be apparent that you probably use most of these strengths from time to time, and this can make them difficult to choose between. The idea is that we can hold around seven concepts or chunks of information in our head at any one time, so it's as good a number as any to focus your attention on the key strengths that energise you and describe you at your best.

Once you're happy with your significant seven, write them down and see if you spot any patterns among them. Do they sit in one or two of the four categories? The Relational and Emotional Strengths are more internal emotional/external people-oriented, whereas the Thinking and Execution strengths are more internal thinking/external task-oriented.

- Is there a theme here?
- How would your friends or colleagues describe you?
- Can you think of any examples that bring these strengths to light?

Think about your current role:

- Do your strengths reflect your role?
- How could you use them more?
- Have your strengths helped you decide on your career path?

… and three standout strengths

But seven strengths are still a lot to hold in our head. There's a saying, usually attributed to Steven Covey of *7 Habits* fame, that 'If you have more than three priorities, you have no priorities'. It's difficult to concentrate fully on more than three of these strengths when faced with a real-life situation.

Identifying your three standout strengths from the seven is useful to ensure that they're always at the back of your mind. Of these seven, choose the three that are most descriptive of you. For each of these strengths, ask yourself these questions (Appendix 12):

- When did I demonstrate this strength?

- How did it help me achieve a successful outcome?
- When and how has it helped me meet a difficult challenge?
- How can I do more of it?

We return to the subject of strengths in Section 4 as we turn our attention to increasing resilience in times of change.

section 3 summary:
change and you: self-awareness

To finish this long section, let's just remind ourselves of the three components of emotional intelligence and use it to summarise where we are:

- **Self-awareness**. The starting point and the focus of this section. This is the ability to recognise your own emotions, when they occur and the reasons for them. You recognise the link between those emotions and your subsequent behaviour, and recognise the impact they may have on others. You know your strengths and your weaknesses, your beliefs and attitudes and whether they help or hinder you.

  We've spent the last four chapters exploring this concept, looking at the various ways we can develop self-awareness and why it's important to do so. We looked at getting feedback, looking through appraisal data themes, self-reflection, coaching and more therapeutic options, mindfulness, motivational drivers, personality characteristics and preferences and, finally, identifying strengths.

- **Self-control**. This is our ability to pass the marshmallow test. People with high self-control can rein in their impulses, say 'No' to themselves and delay gratification because it ends up giving them a better outcome. In times of change, our self-control helps to maintain a positive mindset, remain calm and more focused. We end up being more resilient and self-motivated, able to maintain drive and energy without being prompted or led by others, and to balance short- and long-term goals in the face of rejection or challenge.

  Section 4 explores how we do this.

- **Social awareness**. If self-awareness and self-control are about understanding and being able to deal with your own emotions to get to a satisfactory outcome, then social awareness is about being able to read and deal appropriately with the emotions of others. It's about being able to demonstrate empathic understanding, to show sensitivity and awareness of others' perspectives and being able to respond appropriately to get the best out of a situation.

  Section 5 explores how we can use our self-awareness, self-control and interpersonal skills to take our teams through change.

key learning points

1. The concept of emotional intelligence can help us navigate our way through change. Those with higher emotional intelligence are better able to deal with it.

2. The essence is that of delayed gratification – the ability to say 'No' to yourself. This is about the strength of the link from the emotional part of the brain to the prefrontal cortex, overriding impulse.

3. Emotional intelligence comprises three elements: self-awareness, self-control and social awareness. This essentially means recognising and understanding your own emotions and how to deal with them constructively, and being able to do the same with others' emotions.

4. Self-awareness is our inner rudder. It steers us when we're unsure which way to turn. Developmentally, we need to know where we are before we can get to where we want to go.

5. The more we know ourselves, the more power we have to control ourselves and our reactions.

6. We can raise awareness by some simple practices: getting more feedback from others, reviewing our appraisal data and pulling out themes, self-reflection/diary keeping, obtaining professional help through coaching, counselling or therapy, and by practising mindfulness techniques regularly.

7. Remember the SCARF model – the fast-track to limbic system overload when getting feedback!

8. More in-depth techniques can also help us generate more self-awareness. Understanding our key motivational drivers may help us make decisions on career direction, for example. Understanding our personality variables may help us be aware of our default preferences when approaching tasks or other people.

9. Identifying our strengths and applying them to meaningful pursuits helps us to become our best selves. We look more specifically at how to turn up the dial on your strengths in Section 4.

10. Ultimately, increasing our self-awareness helps us to be clearer about our choices and therefore feel more in control. This is the subject of Chapter 10.

exercises

1. Think about those around you who are successful and happy. What is it about them that makes them successful? How important is their intellectual intelligence? What else could account for their success?

2. How can you get more feedback? From whom? Use or adapt the questions in Appendix 3 and ask those whose opinions you respect.

3. Go back over your last few appraisals using Appendix 4. How useful did you find this? How can you ensure your future appraisals are more useful?

4. Use Appendix 5 to self-reflect on what stressful situations feel like for you and when you start to notice that they're having an impact.

5. Practise the mindfulness exercise in Appendix 7. If you like doing this, get an App such as *Headspace*.

6. Identify your key motivational drivers from Appendix 8. Think about conversations you can have with your boss to make your job look more like your drivers!

7. Look and reflect on the two models of personality given: 16PF™ in Appendix 9 and MBTI© in Appendix 10. If you think it will help, engage the services of a consultant or qualified practitioner to take you through the feedback and implications.

8. Finally, identify your seven significant strengths and then your three standout strengths using Appendices 11 and 12. We return to these in Section 4.

increase your resilience

'There are no facts, only interpretations'
Friedrich Neitzsche

chapter 10

take charge

Section 3 focused on the precursor to increasing your resilience: knowing who you are. What your strengths are. What makes you tick. How you typically react to challenging situations and when your body starts to notice. It's important to know this because what you're aware of, you can control.

self-control

Self-awareness is therefore the first and underpinning component of emotional intelligence. This section concentrates on the second component: self-control – resisting that metaphorical[1] marshmallow to achieve what we want to achieve, and dealing more positively with change.

Life's challenges are rarely as simple as whether or not to eat a marshmallow. It's easy to feel overwhelmed with the usual ups and downs of existence, to get things out of proportion or over-react or, more simply, to get upset about things beyond our control.

---

1   Or real, if you're trying to get control of your weight.

This section follows a simple model that will help to increase your resilience with a view to getting the best possible outcome from sometimes difficult circumstances.[2] We can think of resilience as our ability to cope with and return from life's challenges. It's nothing to do with how far you fall, and everything to do with how well you bounce back.

resilience model

For clarity, we can follow a four-stage model, although in reality we probably do all four of these things simultaneously:

- We take charge. We control what we can control and forget the rest. Easy in principle, but requires some practice in reality!
- We change how we view problems (and ourselves) by what coaches and counsellors call *reframing*.
- We apply our key strengths, motivations and personality preferences to our reframed problem to become 'us on a good day' through forming new habits.
- We ensure that we have support networks in place and that we look after our physical health.

For the rest of this chapter, let's take the first component: take charge.

balance and a sense of proportion

Imagine that you have a friend who phones you every so often to have a good grumble about the state of the world. One week it's the state of the roads, the next week problems in the Middle East, the week after concerns about seemingly unlimited migration.[3] These are all things that we can get cross or concerned about, whether it's too many migrants/refugees, or the way they're being treated (to take a current example in the press as I write this). It's natural and human to feel emotions relating to these events; it also can help us to feel connected to our common sense of humanity, or to our political persuasion.

But it's a question of balance and proportionality – and also whether or not we channel our emotions into action. We're all liable, at times, to get angry or frustrated or upset about things we have no control or influence over. If this is a fleeting emotion, which is proportionate and eventually fades, then this is

---

2   But do think twice before sharing the (often true) statement 'There's no such thing as a problem without a gift for you in its hands'. If someone's in the midst of an amygdala-hijack, you might get punched.

3   People, not swallows.

harmless or maybe even a good thing. It can help us to feel connected, or to get a sense of proportion about our own problems (more of which in Chapter 11).

But when we don't let it go – when we get more and more angry or emotional about things that we have no hope of changing – this is a problem. Eventually, this build-up of stress chemicals such as cortisol can cause us to *feel* stressed, or unhappy, or out of control – with the danger that, at worst, we can spiral down into Seligman's concept of learned helplessness, or even depression.

let it go …

Most of us don't do this, however. But we do often get unhappy or stressed about things that we can't control, and it's amazing how these thoughts and emotions can linger. Our friend, who phones us each week with the voice of doom, may feel temporarily better after a good vent (regardless of the impact on you, however), but ultimately, long-term, they're harming themselves. It can cause unhappiness. And when we're unhappy, we're less resilient. Our problems get out of proportion, and we make poor decisions in other areas of our lives because our thinking becomes more led by our limbic system. One of the first things that reduces with the onset of depression is logical reasoning ability.

Coaches are used to working with this concept. Someone may seek coaching or counselling because they can't see their way through their problems because they seem overwhelming. A coach helps them to identify the parts of the problem they can control, the parts they can't (but may be able to influence) and those aspects that they need to let go of.

So, here we have the nub of the problem. We spend a huge amount of our energy and thought processes on things over which we have no influence, and then let them upset or anger us. Short term, that's probably OK. Longer term, it hurts us. And we do it to ourselves.

… and accept it

Let's be clear about this. The initial feeling, whatever it is and whatever it's about, is OK. It just *is*. We should just accept it. Label it. Understand it. But above all, accept it. You get better at this if you practise mindfulness, as discussed in Chapter 6.

There's no point in wishing things were different. They already are as they are.[4] Nothing can be different from what it already is. We can't change the

---

4   One of my own reframes that I use a lot is 'It is what it is'. No point in wishing it was *already* different. It *already* is.

past or the present moment – only the future. And working out the bit of the future that you can control (usually about you) or influence (other people or the situation) is the trick here. Everything else we put in a box marked 'Let it go'.

circle of control

We can illustrate this in the form of concentric circles (I sometimes draw this for my coaching clients) – see Appendix 13. Take a scenario that's causing you discomfort, stress or unhappiness. In the middle, identify and write down the things that you can control. We may not be able to control the event or other people or the past, but we can control our behaviour and attitudes from this point on. We can control whether we decide to do something or not; our habits and to some extent our thoughts and feelings about the issue. Note what it is that you can control. It is you. Probably *only* you, but you nevertheless.

You may, with action or determined effort or the application of a habit, be able to influence aspects of the situation. These are written in the middle circle. We can't control other people or their reactions, for example, but we can influence them by the way we behave. We may have an influence over certain aspects of a change, for example by forming a lobby group or working party, or using our influencing and persuading skills. Really think hard about this section: we can often influence more than we realise.

Lastly, we identify the things that go in the outer circle: the things we can't control or influence. This could be the essence of the wider change programme, customer expectations, or the past. It is what it is and we are where we are. Worrying unduly and for a long time is not only pointless, it can affect our health. So we need to accept the situation and our feelings about the situation and move on. Remember, we already identified what we choose to influence, so as we've done this the rest just *is*. What you *can* control, of course, is whether you walk away.

really let it go

This is where many of us struggle. As we said above, we can spend a lot of our time, energy and emotions on things we can't do anything about. It's wearing and ultimately pointless. This isn't to say don't have an opinion – on the contrary. But it is about accepting what you can't change and putting your energy towards changing what you can. And if you feel strongly about something, do something about it.

Here's a personal example. Last year (2016), Malta (a beautiful country with mostly lovely people) voted to carry on allowing the shooting of migrating birds going south from Europe for the winter, and again back north from Africa in spring. This is despite intense lobbying and pretty much universal European outcries.[5] It's not really for food. Just sport.

As a keen nature lover, I am of course 'outraged of Berkshire' about this. It's right (for me) that I am. My opinion is based on my personal beliefs and code of ethics, and I 'choose' to be upset and cross about it. But here's the 'but'. Unless I'm prepared to channel my anger into action to try to influence the situation, I have to eventually accept the situation. I don't have to like it, but it is what it is. I wish it wasn't. But it is.

So I have choices. I can sign a petition. I can lobby our government. I can decide not to travel to Malta again until they stop it. But if I choose to do nothing and still allow myself to let my emotions affect me unduly, I'm the one who suffers.[6]

The trouble with focusing on what should already be different, or on things outside our control or influence, is that it's negative. It doesn't do anything. It's reactive. It's harmful to us and ultimately pointless. If we're not careful, we turn ourselves into victims, and the middle circle – what we can control – starts to shrink. The result, at its worst, is learned helplessness – and we've seen that movie before. We don't have to be religious (or an alcoholic, for that matter) to learn from the Alcoholics Anonymous prayer:

> Lord, give me the courage to change the things which can and ought to be changed, the serenity to accept the things which cannot be changed, and the wisdom to know the difference.

So, step 1 is to learn what we can control and what we can't, and to channel our thoughts, feelings and behaviours into the things we can. And, as much as we can, to accept the rest.

Step 2 is to look at how we view the problem, whether we can change how we view it, and how our beliefs and attitudes help or hinder us – so on to the next chapter.

---

5   To be fair, many, many Maltese are pretty upset by this too. The vote was 51% to 49%.

6   Although rather less than the avian community, I guess.

chapter 11

mindset mastery

Let me tell you a story. It's not a very good one, but bear with me. Get yourself comfortable and try to imagine yourself in this position.

a rekindled friendship?

This morning, out of the blue, you have a phone call from an old friend. You haven't heard from her for about five years: no reason, you're just busy people and these things happen. After 10 minutes or so of chatting and catching up, you agree to meet up in a coffee shop this evening at 6pm after work. You put down the phone and get on with your day, really looking forward to seeing your friend this evening. You hope that it's the start of a rekindled friendship.

You leave work slightly early and get to the coffee shop in good time. You snag the two comfortable armchairs by the window and settle down with a drink to wait for your friend. After 15 minutes, your drink's nearly finished and you've read all the leaflets from the last incumbent's magazine. You catch the barista's eye and order another drink, as people are eyeing your comfortable seats with envy and you don't want to get up. You check your phone. You look at your watch: it's now 6.30pm.

You've nothing left to read, so you watch the world go by outside on the street. The coffee shop is getting busy and several people ask you if the spare seat is taken. You manage to cling on to it and carry on waiting. You look at your watch. It's 6.50pm. You wait for another five minutes, then decide to leave. Just as you stand up and gather your belongings, your friend walks through the door ...

Not the most scintillating story, I grant you.[1] But a common enough scenario. Ask yourself the following questions:

- What thoughts went through your head?
- What feelings bubbled up?
- What beliefs about, say, lateness, may have had an impact?
- How might you have behaved when your friend walked in?

typical responses

When I do this exercise in workshops, I usually get a range of responses. You may recognise some of them.

Typical thoughts:

- I wonder if I've got the right time and place?
- I wonder if something's happened to her?
- I hope she's OK.
- She's probably caught in traffic.
- Typical. People are always late for me. It's not fair.
- I hate lateness. How dare she!
- Why can't she let me know where she is? Doesn't she have her mobile with her?
- No wonder we stopped being friends!

Typical feelings:

- Concern
- Worry
- Frustration

---

1   Although if Spielberg hears about this, I claim ownership.

- Annoyance
- Anger
- Betrayal
- Poor me.

All these thoughts and feelings are typical and normal. They just are. You may recognise how you might typically think and feel if you were waiting in the coffee shop. The point is, they're all OK. But the problem is that these absolutely normal thoughts and feelings may affect how you behave when your friend finally walks in. Is this how you would have chosen to behave an hour earlier *to get the result you wanted originally*?

the link with behaviour

Let's say your feelings of concern turn into frustration and then annoyance by the time your friend walks in. How might you then behave? Some of us are able to put our annoyance to one side until we hear the rationale for the lateness, while others may say 'Well, what time do you call this?' or make a point of how long we've been waiting. The tone for the evening has been set:

> You: *'Well, thanks for keeping me waiting! I've been here an hour and it was really embarrassing. You could have let me know.'*

> Her: *'I was caught on the Underground at a points failure. I've been standing for 40 minutes in a hot and packed tube train with no way to contact you. I feel really faint, but thanks for your concern ...'*

The point is, if we're not careful, our behaviour leaks from our thoughts and feelings. The end result may not be what we originally set out to achieve. Think back to the opening scenario: why did we arrange to meet up? *You hope that it's the start of a rekindled friendship.* Not really going to happen now, is it?

And yet we did it to ourselves, when we could've behaved differently. Our thoughts led to our feelings, which led to our behaviour, which created the result. And the result wasn't what we wanted in the first place because of our behaviour. Not to mention our poor friend, who must be feeling a bit frazzled by now!

The trouble is, this is the usual process. We think, we feel, we act and we get a result. It's all rather passive. We end up with what we end up with. And if we have strong beliefs at the front end of this process (which we cover in Chapter 12) it adds a certain strength or direction of travel. If you hate lateness, for example, you're already primed to have more negative thoughts and associated feelings – and a more definite behaviour when your friend actually arrives.

overriding our feelings

There is a remedy, of course. It involves being aware of the thoughts and feelings that surface, stopping them or putting them to one side, and choosing to override them.

In other words, we turn:

(UNEXAMINED BELIEFS) » THOUGHTS » FEELINGS » BEHAVIOUR » RESULT

into

RESULT » BEHAVIOUR » FEELINGS » THOUGHTS » (CHALLENGED BELIEFS)

We can borrow from Steven Covey here. His second habit (from *The 7 Habits of Highly Effective People*) is *Begin with the end in mind*. He means it more as a philosophical position of being in touch with your inner values throughout your life, so you always behave in a way that you'd like people to mention at your funeral,[2] but the principle is the same. Beginning with the end in mind at its simplest means 'Behave in a way that gets the result you want, and dial up thoughts and feelings that help, and dampen down the ones that get in the way'. It means to start with a clear idea of where you want to end up and then working backwards, as illustrated above.

keep the end in mind

Let's go back to our coffee shop example. What's the whole point of being there? What's the end we need to keep in mind? Rekindling an old friendship. As soon as we start to have unhelpful thoughts and feelings, we need to acknowledge them and then let them go. This is why self-awareness is so important: we need to recognise when it starts to happen so we can cool down our hot limbic system. We can then reconnect to why we're there and what we want from the event – and decide to think differently and put any unhelpful thoughts and feelings to one side.

We may decide that if our friend turns up, we'll show concern first and assume that there's a reasonable explanation, and that she probably feels really bad about making us wait. You can then behave sympathetically and there's a greater chance of achieving the end in mind. If she laughs it off and says that she forgot the time because she was browsing in a bookshop, you at least have choices

---

2 Some career coaches use the similar exercise, e.g. 'Write the obituary you want to have' and then coach them into making it happen before they do, actually, need one.

as to how you behave and whether you now still want the original outcome.

So, it's about taking charge again: not of other people, but of the situation and of your thoughts and feelings. It's your own marshmallow test. As we look at later, this system of having a limbic-led urge doesn't always work to our advantage. Going back to the marshmallow studies, the original psychologist, Walter Mischel, said:

> I've watched a pre-schooler's hand suddenly lurch out and hit the bell hard [to end the test and eat the marshmallow], as the surprised child looks down in distress to see what his hand has done.

It's not always easy, but the more control you demonstrate over your thoughts and feelings after the initial limbic push, then the more choices you have – and the more likely you are to get the result you wanted in the first place. You reap what you sow.

take charge of our thoughts and feelings

There's a story about a famous psychologist (George Kelly, if you're interested) that illustrates this. As a therapist, he was working with a rather distressed young woman, and at one point she became extremely agitated and asked Kelly if he thought she was falling apart. At this point, he took off his glasses, leaned forward and replied 'Would you like to?' This was her insight moment. All of a sudden she had a choice. It wasn't inevitable.

It sounds pretty easy, doesn't it? Think of the end result you want, then make sure that your thoughts and feelings help, rather than hinder you. But as we learned in Section 2, when you're in the middle of a hot limbic system wobble, it feels like *it* controls *you*.

Which is why, of course, many of us aren't very good at this. We feel like our emotions control us and we react accordingly. We may even blame them for our behaviour ('Sorry, I was just angry' or 'I can't help feeling like this and it makes me react this way' – or even worse 'It's just the way I am'[3]). But this is the easy way out. We're blaming a part of us for behaving in a way that does us harm.

We use Steve Peters' conceptualisation of this in Chapter 13 when we look at *The Chimp Paradox*, but for now, think of this as a part of us that feels like it isn't. Or, at least, acts like it doesn't want what you originally wanted because it

---

3   To which any psychologist will probably say, in one way or another: 'Or, is it who you choose to be or a habit you've got into? You can change if you want.'

made you behave in a way that made it unlikely to happen. When we realise that we have some control over this process, it helps us to get what we want from whatever situation we find ourselves in.

Let's go back to our brain process again. This is what we said:

Think about our emotions. All an emotion is for is to prompt the body to act in some way – either towards or against something. Once the action is performed, the chemicals – the neurotransmitters we met earlier – gradually dissipate. There's no need for them. The result is that emotions (certainly the initial rush, at any rate) last around 10 to 20 seconds.[4] But of course, they don't. They linger because of our prefrontal cortex, and think about them and the causal event, which generates the neurotransmitter hit all over again ... So we repeat the pattern of thinking and keep on generating the chemical hit, time and time again. We may find ourselves getting angry at the circumstances, other people related or even completely unrelated to the stressful event, or ourselves.

So the trick is to stop the repeating process. We can't do much about the original emotional hit, but after that first one we're doing it to ourselves. And if we're doing it to ourselves, then surely we can control it?

Remember, what we can control is us: we can influence others or the situation. It just doesn't really feel like it. This involves engaging our executive function – the prefrontal cortex-led system, which lets us exert deliberate, conscious control of our thoughts and actions. The more we can make the stressor or temptation abstract and distant from us, the more we should be able to dampen down the urge. Some therapists use the 'fly on the wall' technique to help their clients temporarily see their particular issue from a distance. This can reduce the limbic system's agitation and allow the prefrontal cortex to do its job.

self-awareness

We spent the whole of Section 3 talking about the first step towards controlling our thoughts and feelings. It's self-awareness. What you're unaware of, controls you. Becoming more self-aware, then, is our starting point. The exercise in Appendix 5 will help, as will practising mindfulness. You can also just *notice*. Notice what you feel and when, and ask yourself why. Think about how you react (or are tempted to react), and you can decide to act differently to get the outcome you want. Be kind to yourself – it gets easier with practice. It may help (it helps me, at any rate) to laugh at yourself. It seems to reduce the stress chemicals somewhat.

---

4   With a bit of a lingering after-taste for a while, depending on the particular neurotransmitter.

Don't forget, these chemicals are there to help us survive and make decisions. Our limbic system is continuously having to make *toward* or *away* decisions, depending on our perception of the threat or opportunity. The negative ones, for obvious evolutionary survival reasons, are somewhat stronger: we tend to walk towards, and run away. As we've seen, when this limbic system is aroused, it reduces the resources for rational thought. It's why we can't concentrate under extreme stress so the brain starts acting on default lines, which may or may not be helpful – but are always un-thoughtful.

take control

Our next stage, then, is to carry on getting those hormones and neuro-transmitters under control. Remember, 10 to 20 seconds may be enough to start the calming process so we feel more in control. Some people just take themselves out of the situation and go for a quick walk. This has the added benefit of doing something physical, which helps the chemicals to dissipate more quickly (as if we really were running away from that sabre-toothed cat). Regular exercise as a longer-term strategy is beneficial in lots of ways, of course, as we feel better about ourselves more generally anyway.

Merely trying to suppress the emotion has mixed results. Some of us are good at this, but not many. Our limbic system is stronger than our cognitive processes. It's designed to override them. Trying to suppress emotion in the moment reduces the resources available to us for paying attention in that moment, so we lose track or appear distracted.

There's also a view among some neuroscientists that the healthy and appropriate expression of emotions like anger can have a beneficial effect, by reducing cortisol levels and therefore stress levels. Still others[5] suggest that the rhythm of breathing creates electrical activity in the amygdala and hippocampus. When we breathe in, we stimulate neurons in the limbic system that heighten response times (and memory) and prime us for action – as in quick breathing when we're scared! Slowing breathing down may therefore have a calming effect neurologically.

The problem is that strong emotion hinders cognitive thought, so we can't think straight. We also tend to let it keep repeating on us like a particularly good curry. Anger involves the amygdala and hippocampus, which help us form vivid emotionally charged memories, especially (it now seems) if it makes us

---

5   Paul, M. (2016). 'Rhythm of Breathing Affects Memory and Fear', *Neuroscience News*, 6 December.

breathe more quickly. This causes us to ruminate, like emotional cows chewing the cud of crossness.

amygdala-calming techniques

There are, however, some things we can do in the moment. Even something as simple as counting slowly to 10 and slowing down breathing can be enough. Here's a few more:

- Name six capital cities beginning with the letter A. This may appear (Amsterdam) rather random, but the parts of (Abuja) the brain you use for (Ankara) a cognitive distractor task like this are (Accra) the more logical (Athens) thought and long-term memory parts. The emotions start to calm down enough so you can get them under control (Addis Ababa). You may need to change the letter, though, because if you rehearse and easily remember the capitals, you're not really processing deeply enough for it to be sufficiently distracting. You can also try six words for Red in different languages ... it doesn't really matter what it is. It just has to slow down your limbic system for a while (Asmara).[6]

- Another technique is to label the emotion. It works for the same reason as our first strategy: searching for the right word to label and then explaining the emotion we feel is another cognitive and memory task that can dampen down our limbic system. FMRI scanning has shown that this act actually reduces activity in the amygdala to enable us to get better control.[7] This is somewhat counter-intuitive – studies have shown that people tend to think that labelling an emotion makes things worse. It doesn't. The trick, though, is to use one or two words, not have a discussion with yourself, as this is likely to start the build-up of chemical responses again! All it takes is a second or two.

- Another (situationally suitable) option is to give your limbic system a bit of an airing – in other words, have a good vent! It may only need 5 or 10 minutes of letting off steam to help you get those emotions under control. Obviously, you need to think of the impact this has on others and on your credibility, so do it at the right time in the right place.[8]

---

6   I looked this one up. Don't do this – it's like cheating in a pub quiz. It's not big, funny or clever and it won't calm down your amygdala.

7   Some studies have shown that this is what mindfulness training increases our capacity to do – it effectively increases our ability to shut down the amygdala temporarily.

8   Steve Peters calls this 'exercising the Chimp'.

- Finally, sometimes the mere act of saying to yourself 'I need to put this on the back-burner' is enough to do just that. It's as if you give your brain permission to file it for later. Of course, this short-term repression is just that – short term. You do actually have to address it later or it will linger and fester away.

These are a few techniques to stop the initial amygdala-hijack or limbic system overload. But they are emergency sticking plasters. To be successful in taking charge of our thoughts and feelings, we need to do something more concrete and longer-term – we reframe the problem. Emotions ask the right questions, but the best answers come from cold reason.

reframing

We already met an example of reframing: beginning with the end in mind. When we tell ourselves that we need to focus on the bigger picture or long view, then we're reframing the immediate term. We're using our delayed gratification skills.

When we look at the concept of confirmation bias in Chapter 12, we explore the principle that we look at the world through our own particular and peculiar filters. We don't see the world as it is and we don't see the world as everyone else does. This then affects what we notice and how we think about things, and how we subsequently react.[9]

We borrow from this concept here. Think back to the issue you outlined in Appendix 5. Your conceptualisation of the problem defined it in a certain way and it led, more or less, to the outcomes you illustrated. But this is only one way in which you can define the issue. Reframing is actively choosing to view something differently as a way of dealing with it more positively.

take a different view

So, how else can you view this problem? Have a think and write down at least three other ways you can think about it. For example, redundancy can be viewed as follows:

- The end of employment hopes. On the scrapheap. We're all doomed.[10]
- An opportunity to think about how I want to spend the next 15 years or so of working life.

---

9   I like the Shakespeare quote: 'There is nothing good or bad, but thinking makes it so.' I also like the Anaïs Nin one, which has a similar feel: 'We don't see things as they are, we see them as we are.'

10   This is what your amygdala is trying to get you to think.

- The push I need to go independent.
- An opportunity to get better work-life balance.
- Now I have time to write a book.
- Now's a good opportunity, with redundancy money, to retrain to do what I always wanted to do.

The point is, each view is equally valid. They are all true for any given definition of *true*. And we can choose the one we want that helps us. Reframing is changing the way we think about something: to look for the silver lining in the cloud of despondency, to see the threat as an opportunity. Sensible balance is called for, of course, but the essence of reframing is that we're choosing only one way (of many) of looking at the issue in the first place. Your brain already chose without you, as it were.

At the time of writing, one of the worst events that's ever happened to me, happened. This week, someone stole my wheelie-bin. I know, I feel your waves of empathic understanding. It is, of course, mildly annoying and meant I had to call the local authority and everything. My brain, of course, sees this as a threat to my sense of fairness (think SCARF again), so I'm annoyed.

There's no point staying annoyed, though. No-one wins. So a reframe involves getting a sense of perspective (other people have slightly more pressing problems, to be honest) and to find the positive from it (a new anecdote for this book, and a shiny new bin). And to let go of the rest, because, you know, it will get sorted.

Later we use the chimp model to help us reframe. Before we do, there's one more piece of the jigsaw to address.

unexamined beliefs

We talked about the usual flow of events:

(UNEXAMINED BELIEFS) » THOUGHTS » FEELINGS » BEHAVIOUR » RESULT

And we turned them into:

RESULT » BEHAVIOUR » FEELINGS » THOUGHTS » (CHALLENGED BELIEFS)

and how we can better manage our initial thoughts and feelings to make our behaviour get the result we originally wanted. The one bit of this equation we haven't talked about is the (Unexamined) beliefs part, and this is quite fundamental to the whole process.

Our beliefs (about the world, about other people, about ourselves) front-load everything, and they influence the original way you view your challenging issue by determining your default. As a cause of unhappiness, and the subsequent remedy, it's the big one. Our beliefs and associated attitudes have the biggest impact on our performance at work and our behaviour in general; and there's a problem. We don't behave like scientists do. And we often can't explain why we have the beliefs we do. We just do.

And, boy, can we believe some things.[11] It's possible that some of you believe that we're all haunted by the spirits of aliens who originally came to earth in giant spaceships some 75 million years ago, and who were then subsequently massacred by a galactic warlord called Xenu using hydrogen bombs.

It's entirely possible you believe this because, according to the organisation itself that believes it, 30 million others do. Including Tom Cruise and John Travolta. Yep, it's one of the central tenets of Scientology. Of course, it may be true. Or, it may have been made up by a madman with no evidence whatsoever apart from a rather vivid dream after eating too much cheese. You decide.

When it comes to beliefs, sometimes logic and rational thought take a holiday. Let's explore this a bit more because it has a direct link to our own resilience.

---

11   Subjective opinion alert.

chapter 12

the big lie

OK, not a lie exactly. But not necessarily truth either. This chapter is about beliefs and their part in our story.

Let me start by telling you three more stories.

planetary determinism

A friend invited me round to their garden last summer and said something like:

> Just look at my garden. Everything I plant just dies. I spend £100 every couple of months but, after a few weeks everything's dead. I really don't know why I bother.
>
> Mind you, I don't know why I'm surprised. I am a Gemini.[1]

Right. I may now be alienating a certain percentage of my audience[2] but it's a risk worth taking because it is sort of the point. There's no evidence that the position of the stars and planets when we're born has any link to our horticultural dexterity. No evidence whatsoever. Yet it's a belief that many,

---

1   Cue *totally bewildered face*.

2   About 25% of you, according to The Independent in 2011.

many people have and a belief system that finds its way into most newspapers and magazines. It helps some people make sense of the world by attaching a meaning to random events, and it gives some people comfort. But the point is, there's no reliable scientific evidence and some people change their behaviour because of it. Such beliefs are not harmless, and this is why.

My friend believes that Geminis can't garden. This is a belief that helps create her attitudes and leaks into her thoughts and feelings. As we saw in Chapter 11, thoughts and feelings affect behaviour. Which creates the result.

If my friend believes Geminis can't garden, she won't try as hard or will forget to water her plants, because her beliefs tell her that there isn't much point – because Geminis can't garden. See how circular this becomes? It gets worse. Because now everything's died, her original belief is reinforced. She has the evidence. No-one can tell her any differently.[3]

Of course, horoscopes trade on ambiguity and our desire to search for meaning. They're written in a way that enables us to attach a specific meaning based on what we already expect to see. What you seek, you will find. What you expect (or hope) to see, you will see.

Here's a real example from a newspaper this year, together with my commentary in italics:

Aries (21 Mar to 20 Apr)

It's a good idea to get into work mode and move away from distracting adventures. *When isn't it? The clue's in the word* distracting ... *Anyway, imagine the howls of protest if it said the opposite.*

However, this week's Mars/Uranus aspect can keep you wanting and waiting for something exciting to happen. *Erm, when aren't we? Who would say no to that?*

Just keep your mind sharp and be prepared to compromise. *What? Erm, OK then. 'Cos normally I wouldn't find it useful at all, would I!*

You get the picture. But this isn't just trivial horoscope-bashing. If we feel that we're mere pawns determined by the position of the planets, we feel powerless to control our lives and stop trying to have an impact or do things differently. Ultimately, it can stop us trying and lead to learned helplessness.

It doesn't have to be about horoscopes. In our coffee shop example, if our pre-existing belief is that people shouldn't be late, this will start to leak into our thoughts and feelings, which create our behaviour – which turned into

---

3   Especially me, being Pisces.

the result we didn't want. If we believe that we're not the sort of person who can (insert what you can't do *yet* here), then this self-limiting belief ultimately becomes a self-fulfilling prophecy. Our beliefs about ourselves and the way the world works are ultimately the major influence on our resilience.

close encounters of the first kind

That's correct: there's more than just the third kind.[4] Starting from the most extreme, close encounters of the fourth kind are actual alien abduction, the third kind direct contact (as in the film), the second is a sighting supported by direct evidence and the first kind is a sighting with no supporting evidence.

Now obviously the first kind is the most common. By far. And it's a phenomenon which suffers from the sort of cognitive biases we discuss in this chapter.[5] Most (though, of course, not all) sightings are by people who are interested in the subject of aliens and who often look for them, or at least are alert to the possibility. What we look for, we find. What we expect to see, we see – or at least misinterpret the data to fit in with our expectations.

Both our memories and our perceptions are what psychologists call top-down processes – they're constructed, not passive, processes and are greatly affected by our pre-existing beliefs and what we expect to see. Add this process of constructed perception to poor viewing conditions, a sky with no nearby size cues (a small, near and slow-moving object looks the same to your retina as a large, distant and fast-moving one[6]) and we have the finding that over 95% of reported sightings can be explained by this process. The usual culprits are aircraft seen from unusual angles, weather conditions, Chinese lanterns and meteors. But it's not how it feels. And we take some convincing that our belief in what we think we've seen is a misinterpretation. This doesn't mean, of course, that aliens don't exist. It's impossible to prove a negative. It's just that we don't act like scientists.

being a scientist

There are only two things I remember from the Research Methods module of my undergraduate Psychology degree. The first is that correlation doesn't

---

4   There's no truth in the rumour that the others joined once the third kind became famous.

5   This has nothing to do with a belief as to whether aliens exist or not. I'm with the vast majority of scientists who find it hard to accept that we're alone in the universe. This is a story about evidence.

6   As parodied by Father Ted: 'One last time, Dougal. These are small (toy) cows, but the ones out there are far away.'

imply causation – itself often a cognitive bias. Just because two things tend to have a relationship, it doesn't follow that one causes the other – yet we often believe it to be so. People change their lottery numbers if a number comes up the previous week, somehow assuming that the balls have a memory and are therefore less likely to come up again. Sunshine and ice-cream sales are correlated, but I'm not sure that ice-cream sales cause the sun to shine.

Anyway, the other thing I remember is what the scientific method actually is once you strip away all the clever bits – and this is important for our journey in this chapter because it's sort of the remedy.

Imagine that you're a scientist and invent a drug that appears at first testing to cure short-sightedness. You're going to make a fortune.[7] Your whole career and not a small amount of fame ride on this discovery. You design a set of experiments to try to prove your hypothesis that your drug actually does cure short-sightedness.

Well, actually, you don't, if you're a proper scientist. Somewhat counter-intuitively, you try to do the opposite. You design a series of experiments that try to prove what the scientific method calls the *null* hypothesis – that the drug has no demonstrable effect. You then get your peers (through a process called peer review) to do the same. If you, and they, can't prove it doesn't work, you accept to a degree of probability that it does.

Remember the discovery of the Higgs-Boson, or god-particle – the particle that appears to give objects mass? The scientists at CERN thought they may have found it in the Large Hadron Collider, so they kept on and on trying to break the data to prove they hadn't. They then gave the data to the whole scientific community, saying 'We can't break it – can you?'

the scientific method

Why does the scientific method insist on this? It's primarily to avoid the traps told by the first two stories in this chapter. Memory and perception are constructed from pre-existing beliefs, and our brains are very clever at proving what we already believe.

Without looking now, what do you think the picture is on the front cover of this book? If you've read this far you've seen it several times. Based on your experience of the book's subject matter, I don't mind betting you assumed, at least initially, that it was a brain cell. If you did, then you let your experiences (of the book) or your subsequent expectations of the content affect your interpretation

---

7   And possibly be on the 'unfortunate accident' hitlist of spectacle manufacturers.

of a slightly ambiguous image. It is, in fact, a photograph I took of a hole in the harbour-ice in Stockholm. The point is, this is how our memory and perception works. Everything else leaks into them, including what we want or expect to find.

This process can be both conscious and (more often) unconscious, but the point is it feels right and no-one will be able to convince you otherwise. If we expect to find something, our brains interpret the evidence to support our expectations. We don't usually act like scientists and try to prove the null hypothesis.[8]

For further evidence of the (irrational) beliefs affecting behaviour en masse, this bit of research was published in the press just today: Zoopla's research shows that houses at number 13 in the street are, on average, £9,000 cheaper because of superstition about the number. Utter, utter madness.

One extra little cupcake in the pantry of evidence-based thought is also a little depressing. It even has a name – the Dunning-Kruger effect. It's a simple concept: the less intelligent we are, the more confident in our beliefs we tend to be. Let that roll around your prefrontal cortex for a moment. The point is that recognising your own limitations and irrational beliefs involves intelligence. Countering this argument is that the more intelligent we are, the more able we are to find the evidence to support our existing beliefs – so we can't really win.

There is, of course, a name for this process and it's a very important process indeed. It affects probably everything we do and believe. There are even some writers who suggest that who we are as an adult is made up of three things: our genetic make-up, our environmental upbringing and the sum total of the lies we've told ourselves that have become our truth.

It's called *confirmation bias*, and it's at the heart of our ability to increase our resilience.

confirmation bias: the big lie

Confirmation bias works like this. Pretty early on in our lives, we form a set of principles and beliefs about ourselves, our place in the world and how the world works. This comes from our immediate family, our religion, the politics of our parents, our social class, the part of the world we're brought up in, the way we're schooled and a myriad of other influences.

These beliefs helped us make sense of things when, intellectually, the 'facts'

---

8   In an interview with *The American Atheist*, Douglas Adams – *The Hitchhiker's Guide to the Galaxy* author – suggests: 'All opinions are not equal. Some are a very great deal more robust, sophisticated, and well-supported in logic and argument than others.'

and any analytical thinking were beyond us. But we tend not to revisit them as an adult. We look for evidence to support the beliefs we've built up and ignore or rationalise any evidence to the contrary. We even remember facts that support our existing beliefs better, too. These beliefs are therefore reinforced – we've skewed the evidence to fit with what we already believe. All a hammer ever sees is a nail.[9]

Here's an example. I recently did some development work with teachers at a large Further Education College. One of the issues they constantly address is that many of their pupils believe that they can't do maths. If all your young life you're told you're no good at maths, it comes to define you. You start telling yourself 'I'm not the sort of person who can do maths', and this self-limiting belief becomes a self-fulfilling prophecy because – just like Geminis can't garden – it leaks into your confidence, thoughts and feelings and, ultimately, behaviour and results. You are *now* not good at maths because challenging your brain's ingrained belief is harder than dealing with the failure.

So we get into a negative thinking loop and don't try as hard, or don't try at all. And, of course, we have a lifetime's evidence to back up this belief. It's amazing, though, how inserting the word 'yet' into 'I can't do maths' can make a difference.[10]

negativity bias

Just to add an extra frisson to this, we're actually far more likely to remember the negative over the positive: we have an inbuilt negativity bias. It used to help us survive by focusing on problems. Now it tends to reduce our resilience by sucking the fun out of the world around us. Negative emotions reduce our happiness and wellbeing more than positive ones increase them.[11] Focusing on quick fixes – like a shopping trip – work for a short time, then it's back to how it was before.

The essence, then, of confirmation bias is that the brain is very reluctant to change its mind. Once it forms beliefs, it takes a huge amount of effort to disbelieve. So, most of the time, we don't. The absence of control creates anxiety, so holding on to beliefs gives us that control – if only control of our beliefs. And those beliefs were originally formed by skewing the evidence – we constructed our perception and memory from among a sea of data by

---

9   My favourite confirmation bias joke is from the journalist Jon Ronson: 'Ever since I first found out about confirmation bias, I've been seeing it everywhere.'

10 If, like me, you are obsessed with the Paralympics, you see this in every athlete. This is real 'Take charge and master your mindset' territory.

11 People with depression pay far more attention to negative stimuli, so of course it seems real; everything positive is downplayed and everything negative is TRUE.

choosing which bits to pay attention to. Memory also has an ego – we tend to remember things that made us look and feel good and then believe them.

Of course, as my namesake Will Storr in his book *Heretics* mentions, the real world is out there. It's just not the version you're seeing or believing. Those are just the bits you've made up to make sense of the data. Efficiency is the key word here. Your brain uses up a lot of resources, so it constantly strives to reduce this cognitive load and drain on energy by repeating patterns, scripts, schemas and pre-existing beliefs so it doesn't have to reinvent the wheel. We make it up. We're so heavily reliant on what we already know that we don't tend to unlearn it.

information overload

Part of the problem, of course, is that there's so much information out there. We'd go mad if we tried to attend to all of it. Some writers (Professor John Grey, for example, in *Straw Dogs*) suggest that we receive 14 million bits of information per second. So we have to choose. And we choose what we already know and believe in. Being exposed to a mixed body of evidence tends to make us more convinced of the validity of our original beliefs. Neurologically, confirming existing beliefs activates reward circuits in the brain so that it feels good. So we do more of it, while denying to ourselves that we're doing it.[12]

The point to all of this is, not just that we all do it, but that it's usually invisible to us. We can't climb out of our head and look objectively at our prejudices and beliefs, because they're usually unconscious. Many organisations run unconscious bias training to ensure this doesn't affect selection during a recruitment process, for good reason. We're all biased. And as we said in Chapter 11:

> Our beliefs (about the world, about other people, about ourselves) front-load everything, and they influence the original way you view your challenging issue by determining your default.

Our brains decide for us what's real and what's not based on our experiences, so if we grow up in a particular belief system or culture, our brains conclude that it is 'real' and 'true'. Shifting this is hard, so not many people do it.

If this all sounds hopeless, it is. Well, not quite. If you believe a lucky rabbit's foot helps you do well in an interview, then this belief may give you enough confidence to perform better, despite it not being very lucky for the rabbit. It's not going to help you win the lottery, though. This is the placebo effect in action.

However, these beliefs can limit us unduly. It's hopeless a lot of the time if we don't challenge our beliefs and act more like scientists.

---

12 We even have a Bias bias, in which we 'know' we're less biased than the average biased person.

what this means for our resilience

This is where we merge the last two chapters. In Chapter 11, we talked about our need to turn:

(UNEXAMINED BELIEFS) » THOUGHTS » FEELINGS » BEHAVIOUR » RESULT

into

RESULT » BEHAVIOUR » FEELINGS » THOUGHTS » (CHALLENGED BELIEFS)

if we want to take charge of a situation – if we don't want to end up with a result we didn't necessarily want. We talked about starting with the end in mind – the results we actually want from a situation – and making sure our behaviours, thoughts and feelings support, not hinder, that result.

Think about the patterns you typically demonstrate in your thoughts, feelings and behaviours. Do they help? If not, then maybe starting with the result will. This is the first bit. The second bit is to challenge these beliefs about ourselves or our situation to ensure the self-limiting belief doesn't become the self-fulfilling prophecy. Which leads us right back to self-awareness: knowing what these beliefs are is a pre-requisite for challenging them.[13] That of which you're unaware controls you, remember!

look through a different lens

The analogy I draw in my training sessions on increasing resilience is going to the optician to get your eyes tested. The optician will put on your nose an empty frame with lots of grooves or slots in it. She will then put one, two, maybe three lenses in those slots at a time, changing what you see through each lens. Sometimes things seem blurred, other times crystal clear. But what you see is an interpretation, light from whatever object you look at refracted and bent by the lenses to change it in some way.

This is a good analogy for how we're born. We are (mostly) born with no worldview or belief systems about ourselves or how the world works; then our parents, our local society, our culture, the religion of our family and our experiences put a set of lenses in that empty frame on our nose. We now look at the world through all those lenses, yet – and here's the big problem – we call what we see through those lenses *Reality*.

It's no such thing. It's a construct based on our life. It's Plato's projection

---

13 I've met many, many people who seem to confuse 'want' with 'need', and this thinking frame ultimately affects your beliefs about how the world 'should' work, leading to a reduction in happiness when it inevitably doesn't. Likewise is a belief in a 'just' world, despite evidence to the contrary. The world just is. You're only ever going to be either disappointed or end up delusional.

on to the cave wall. Everyone's projection is different. But we insist ours is right and don't re-evaluate it. And it can bind us. This set of beliefs affects you and me right now by selecting what we notice, changing what we do notice and affecting how we interpret what we notice.

facts vs beliefs

We can get very confused by what actually *is* a fact. Of course, it's a fact that the sun and the moon are the same size. It's obvious. During an eclipse, there's virtually perfect covering of the sun by the moon. And an awful lot of people believe that this is the truth. However, the fact – supported by a wide range of evidence from a multitude of disciplines – is that this is mere coincidence; the moon is 400 times smaller than the sun and, bizarrely, 400 times nearer. Hence, they look the same size.

Here are a few more facts:

- Hot water freezes faster than cold water.
- Swallows hibernate in the bottom of ponds for the winter.
- The earth is flat.

All of these used to be facts, i.e. widely known as true. Now, none of them are. The facts haven't changed. Our evidence and knowledge has.

These beliefs can either help or hinder us. Resilient people recognise the beliefs that hinder them, challenge them by looking for evidence, and gradually change their belief through reframing and evaluating this evidence until a more helpful belief replaces it. *I can't* into *I can't yet but I can try*, maybe.

challenging our belief systems

An example may help here. Imagine that you believe (and have done as long as you can remember) in fate and destiny. You believe that there's a time ordained when you're going to die, whenever you meet people it's for a reason and 'meant to be', and all life's events are pretty much pre-determined.

I've met many people with this belief system. One explanation is that our brains don't like the concept of randomness. It's used to trying to see patterns so it finds them when they're not there: the consequence is the belief that everything happens for a reason or is somehow pre-chosen. Obviously, at some level this demands that someone or something is doing the pre-ordaining, but regardless, it's a belief that many people share. You spend your life confirming this belief to yourself by interpreting evidence after the event: 'I *knew* that person was sent for a reason' and 'It wasn't meant to happen'. These are ways that make us feel good (or at least better) because they confirm our belief system. It all stays unchallenged.

What we then do is start cherry-picking this evidence. When something good happens, it's fate and destiny. It was meant to happen. (*Subtext: it* wasn't *down to me.*) When something bad happens, we blame ourselves and say we deserve it or are repaying past debt. (*Subtext: it* was *down to me.*) It doesn't take long for this skewing of the evidence, this cherry-picking, to lower our confidence and even self-esteem. And what's particularly sad is that we do it to ourselves. It's very hard to convince someone else that their deeply held views are irrational or wrong, or that there's little evidence for them.

The only remedy, therefore, is self-awareness (that this is what you're doing) and to start questioning your belief system. What's your evidence? Do you look when you cross the road? Why, if your fate isn't in your hands? It won't help you if that belief is true, so maybe, just maybe, it isn't – and you don't really believe it.

Then we can really start to challenge ourselves to think differently; to take out the lens of 'destiny' and replace it with one of 'self-empowerment' instead. Our new way of looking at the world becomes one of making our own fate – an external locus of control. And the more power we feel we have to affect the world and our own lives, the more resilient we become. It just takes practice. Once we're an adult, we can replace the lens.

One final point here. It doesn't actually matter whether there *is* such a thing as fate or destiny. You'll never know for sure. You behave according to one of those beliefs anyway. It's less important to find any objective reality (which may or may not exist[14]) than to question the things you tell yourself that get in the way of happiness – or resilience, or work performance, or your journey through a change process – and change them.

And I reckon that if you look hard enough, you can find a Gemini who's good at gardening.

---

14   Ask any Quantum theorist, if you can find one who actually exists.

13

of fish!, chimps and elephants

If the last chapter sounded a bit negative, then it wasn't meant to. If you're struggling with resilience at the moment, it may be that your beliefs aren't helping you, so once you start to unpick them, it will all be fine. You just need to challenge them.

Daniel Kahneman has written extensively (his award-winning book *Thinking, Fast and Slow*, for example) about this process. We think we're rational, but it's the thinking fast (emotional brain) that evaluates evidence first, and then the thinking slow (rational thought) tends to search for evidence to validate the feeling. We get the hunch, and make up (or selectively notice) the facts afterwards to reinforce the hunch. And think we've been objective. We told ourselves a story, and we then filled in the script afterwards.

Because we seem wired to respond positively to stories, many books on dealing resiliently with change are written as parables. *Who Moved My Cheese?*, for example.[1] Here are three that involve animals. Because, well – just because it works.

---

1   And the sequels *Who Keeps Moving My Bloody Cheese?, Get Your Own Cheese If You Like It That Much* and *It's Just Not Gouda Nuff: You'd Better Tread Caerphilly*. You're welcome.

fish!

Although not specifically about resilience per se, this short book is about change, improving morale and taking charge. It's a parable set in Seattle about learning to love what you do – and how it's ultimately completely up to you. The central premise is that you can choose your attitude.

A new manager takes over an unproductive team who have poor morale, a bad work ethic and just look downright miserable.[2] This leaks into their customer service (remember the ATTITUDE–THOUGHTS–FEELINGS–BEHAVIOUR–RESULTS link we discussed previously) so they get bad feedback and a worse reputation in the company. Our heroine is sent in to turn it around.

Initially at a loss what to do, she visits Pike Place fish market and sees fishmongers, up to their elbows in cold smelly fish guts, having a whale (sorry) of a time, bantering with the customers and attracting a lot of business. The atmosphere is one of lightness, joy of life and everything her office, frankly, isn't.

She learns one powerful lesson on this visit. The attitude we bring to anything (here, her team's attitude to their work) is something we create. We choose it. We can choose to have a miserable time at work in what she calls the toxic energy dump, or we can choose to be different.

We've all met these people. Psychic Vampires. Mood Hoovers. Dementors, if you work at Hogwarts. So, this is where *Fish!* chimes with this book. We can choose the attitude we bring to change. Everything, ultimately, is a choice.

beliefs vs attitudes

Let's explore this a little more. We can't choose our beliefs. This may sound odd after everything I said in the last chapter, but it's sort of true. You can't suddenly decide to believe in Father Christmas, or the Tooth Fairy, or horoscopes. You either do or you don't. We can challenge our beliefs once we identify them, and eventually may change them, but the change in our belief is a by-product of our thinking and evidence gathering and mulling it over and chatting it through – and eventually, maybe, just maybe, the belief changes into something else.

This is how *beliefs* are different from *attitudes*. We can change our beliefs with effort. Or they may change by themselves. But we can change – and choose – our attitudes in a heartbeat. You choose the attitude you take to a meeting, to a training course, to a Monday morning, to a change process.

---

2   I bet you have a work colleague in your head now.

It may not always feel it, but it's always a choice.[3]

If anything, choosing your attitude is what Section 4 of this book is all about. Instead of letting your attitude rule (and inhibit) you, take charge of it. Own it. Decide whether it helps you, and change it if it doesn't. You can unpick your deeper beliefs later, but choosing your immediate attitude can be as simple as telling yourself to get a grip and be positive, if you want it to be.

Understanding this, then, is helped by knowing one of the founding principles of cognitive behavioural therapy: our reactions (behaviours as a result of thoughts and feelings) are not caused by events, but by our thoughts (and ultimately, beliefs) about those events and a later interpretation of what they mean.

This isn't a new idea. Epictetus (writing in the Stoic traditions about 2,000 years ago) suggested that what upsets us is not the thing itself but our judgement about that thing. This puts the onus firmly and squarely on us. In his own words:

> We have no power over external things, and the good that ought to be the object of our earnest pursuit, is to be found only within ourselves.

choosing our attitude

The remedy, therefore, is what we've been suggesting all along. Choosing our attitude is a simple three-stage process:

1. Become aware of the thoughts and feelings you're having about a situation, and try to identify any beliefs about that situation you're telling yourself. Remember that what you're unaware of controls you, so bringing these thoughts, feelings and beliefs into awareness means you can ultimately control (and change) them. They usually reside in the murky undergrowth; bring them out into the open. Keeping a diary might also help this process, as we discussed in Section 3. It may be easier at first to do this retrospectively. The exercise given in Appendix 5 is meant to help you do this. The act of writing it all down often helps reduce the emotional content. Eventually, you'll become aware of your thinking habits, whether they be a tendency to catastrophise ('This is awful and we're all doomed'), over-generalise ('It always happens to me; I'll never get this), being overly judgemental of yourself and/or others ('I'm hopeless; they shouldn't be doing that), mind-read ('They think I'm useless') or predict the future ('If I do this, then that is bound to happen').

2. Challenge your unhelpful thinking habits and beliefs. Be a scientist. What

---

3   I say this to my delegates; they choose the attitude they bring into the training room – openness to learn, waste of time, gets me out of a meeting ... and each one creates its own outcome and becomes its own truth.

is the truth? What would someone else notice? What are facts and what are assumptions?[4] It may help to pretend you're a lawyer presenting the case for and the case against. Ask yourself what evidence you have, what other interpretations there might be and if there are any other possible outcomes than the one you imagined. The more you get into the habit of doing this, the easier it will become. The worksheet in Appendix 14 will help.

3. Create new, more helpful thoughts. Let them replace the old, unhelpful ones. You may be able to focus on the positive, such as asking yourself: What's gone well?, What strengths can help me? (Chapter 9), Who can help me?, What's the most important thing in this scenario? and What can I learn from this? Have I got the right perspective? Is there a positive I can find in this? It may help to think of such problems as temporary, only affecting a small part of your life or that there are many causes, not just you, of this event.

chimps

In Section 2, we looked at the structure of the brain, the order in which it developed and the modern-day consequences of having a system that's hundreds of thousands of years old, which developed to help us survive a wild animal attack:

- The oldest bit (hindbrain) notices threat or opportunity.
- The middle bit (limbic system and memory) generates an emotional response leading to fight, flight or freeze to respond to the attack.
- And then, and only maybe, we pass it through the youngest bit of the brain (the neocortex, the bit that makes us human) to apply logic, proportionality and rational thought to it.

Maybe. The implication is that we can tend to treat change as a threat and we then generate the threat response – or even the bereavement response, as change always seems to involve loss of some kind. The argument for explaining this model is that it can help to make sense of the (often) illogical or disproportionate feelings and therefore *behaviours* we demonstrate when someone steals our stapler. Even the smell of rotting fish can trigger our fight/ flight mechanism, as our olfactory centre of the brain is located pretty close to the amygdala, so the signals can leak.

This brain structure is the starting point for Professor Steve Peters' book

---

4   Often confused, and a fact usually ends up being an assumption, or at least an interpretation. There aren't many facts around.

The Chimp Paradox.[5] He uses exactly the same model as above, but just gives things more user friendly names:

- Our limbic system (including the amygdala, our emotional memory centre), he renames our *Chimp*.
- Our prefrontal cortex, our logical rational part, he calls our *Human*.
- And the beliefs, habitual thinking patterns and ultimately, attitudes, all reside as lines of code in our *Computer*.

In this way, Peters links our brain biology and structure with the cognitive behavioural remedies mentioned above in the Fish! section.

Let's take your inner Chimp, your limbic system, first. Peters likens it to a chimp because it's fast and strong (around seven times faster and stronger than your Human (logical thought)). So there's no point in trying to fight it. It will win. Emotion trumps logic every time. It's concerned with whatever it is that chimps are concerned with. Status. Territory. The troop. Resources. Ego. It works on instinct, is focused on survival and is your 'thinking fast' state. And the major implication for this model, and Peters' basic premise, is that your Chimp thinks independently from you (your Human). And that's not always in your best interests – hence the title of the book. The paradox is that the Chimp is you but not you, and its agenda is different to yours.[6]

Your Human is you, or at least the 'you' that you're usually aware of. It is your thoughts, your logic, your rational self and your thinking slow state. It focuses on facts, seeks the truth and applies logic to them.

Your Computer, however, is accessed by both the Chimp and the Human. It is where your scripts, thinking habits and typical ways of responding reside. It contains helpful programmes (such as positive self-talk, positive attitudes and beliefs) which Peters calls Autopilots, and unhelpful programmes (negative self-talk, negative attitudes and self-limiting beliefs) which he calls Gremlins.

Peters' model

So, that's the model. It's no different from the spirit of this book but it gives a framework to the technical aspects of brain function that many people find helpful. It works like this.

---

5   Peters is a Psychiatrist who's helped many famous athletes such as Chris Hoy, Victoria Pendleton and Ronnie O'Sullivan with mindset management.

6   Peters suggests you give your Chimp a name to make the point that it's not really you. You're responsible for what your Chimp does, but not how it feels. You can learn to manage it.

Some external stimulus, such as a conversation, an action from someone else, or a change, happens. It hits our Chimp first (thinking fast) who quickly looks into the Computer to see what programmes are there to tell it how to behave. It then reacts by attempting to protect or fight, depending on what Gremlins are in the Computer. Examples of Gremlins might be:

- I'm too old to change.
- Things should stay as they are.
- I have no control over my feelings.
- I'm not capable/worthy.
- I have no power.
- I can't help it.
- It's just who I am.

Whatever Gremlins are programmed into the Computer adds to the already hyper-sensitive Chimp, who's focused on survival at all costs. The result is inappropriate explosions of anger, negative thought spirals, feelings of hopelessness and negativity or unhelpful attitudes.

The stimulus eventually gets to our Human, who also looks into the Computer. If it finds the same Gremlins, it uses logic and rational thought to justify the Chimp's actions. (We called this confirmation bias.) It may also be too late, because the Chimp has made you storm out of the meeting, or be unnecessarily aggressive, or behave with a negative, despondent 'poor me' attitude.

what to do next

The remedy, then, is two-fold.

Firstly, we have to manage the immediate agitation of the Chimp. Don't forget, it's strong and fast and (effectively) illogical – at least, in today's setting – so you can't fight it. Emotion trumps logic. So we need to learn to manage it. It needs to be let out of its box, but appropriately: in other words, you may be able to take yourself out of the situation and walk around to give your Chimp a talking-to, or let it express itself by having a bit of a vent. It often needs just 10 minutes of airtime. But the point is, we can put off that airtime until we're out of the meeting, or away from the conversation.

Remember we mentioned in Section 2 that emotions last a matter of seconds, so using distractor tasks that we identified in Chapter 11 may help (counting to 10, naming six capital cities beginning with F, etc). Sometimes, just saying to yourself 'I intend to put this away for later' actually enables us to do so – but we do need to go back to it or it will fester.

Secondly, we need to go back to reframing, which in Peters' model is called 'turning the Gremlins to Autopilots'. It's pretty much what we mentioned earlier in Chapter 11. We need to know what our Gremlins are – those unhelpful thoughts, attitudes and beliefs – and question them. If we decide they don't help us (which is, by definition, a Gremlin) then we replace this unhelpful thought, attitude or belief with a helpful one.

Again, it doesn't matter too much whether it's actually true or not. The point is, with practice and through confirmation bias, this time working *for* us, it will become true. Mindful practice is key here. Recognise the Gremlin, practise turning it into an Autopilot and eventually it will become, well, automatic.

Some examples of Autopilots are:

- Security is relative.
- No-one likes a victim-mentality.
- You can choose your attitude.
- No-one owes me anything.
- Yes, I can (Paralympics slogan from 2016).
- It is what it is and we are where we are.
- No point in wishing things were already different.
- I can manage my feelings.
- Happiness is a choice.
- You can only take, not give, offence.

So, applying this to change, we can create some change-related Autopilots to practise. Eventually we'll believe them, and our Chimp will grumble a bit and get back in the box. Here are some:

- We're never fully secure; life is transient.
- I've dealt with change all my life.
- I may not like it, but I can change.
- How important is this to the rest of my life?
- There are things I can, and things I can't control.
- There's risk in not changing.
- I can always walk away.

This last one is important and empowering. You always have the choice to walk away. Just do it as the result of an Autopilot your Human has evaluated, not because your Chimp is telling you to run away.

One final idea. One way of catching our Chimp off-guard is to make it laugh. Laughing at yourself, and your reactions, makes the Chimp feel less stressed. Talk to your Chimp in an accent. Tell it a joke. Recognise that someone on the outside may find the situation quite amusing. We are all, after all, when you think about it, completely and utterly ludicrous.

elephants

The final example in our vertebrate trilogy is the work of Chip and Dan Heath in their book *Switch*. Or more accurately, *Swıtch*.[7]

They argue that there are three surprises about change:

- What looks like a people problem is often a situation problem. Provide people with smaller buckets of popcorn, they eat less. Behaviour changes.
- Often, the heart and mind disagree. This is a tension going all the way back to Plato, and is at the heart of *The Chimp Paradox* above.
- What looks like resistance is often a lack of clarity.

Therefore, their model addresses these three surprises.

So where does the elephant come in? In the Heaths' model, the elephant is pretty much the same as Peters' Chimp. The elephant is our emotional side (our limbic system) and our rational side (our Human in Peters' model and mostly our pre-frontal cortex) is the elephant's rider. You already see where this is going, don't you?

The rider's control of the elephant is precarious due to their difference in size and strength; whenever there's disagreement (usually, according to surprise number two above), then there's only going to be one winner, just like our Chimp is much stronger than our Human. It's the elephant that refuses to go to the gym (because elephants are lazy) when the rider wants to because it's good for you (and has good intentions), and it's the elephant which has that first marshmallow. The elephant is looking for immediate satisfaction, whereas the rider is concerned with longer-term goals. If you want to change, you have to appeal to both: the elephant gets things done while the rider procrastinates, and eventually the rider provides the planning and direction.

---

7   See what they did there?

willpower

There's an interesting parallel with a concept we mentioned elsewhere:[8] self-control. Self-control, or willpower, is a finite resource. You exert willpower in one area of your life, and there's less left over for others. There's quite a lot of research evidence for this. Politicians exert it in one direction (their career, for example), but may not have much left over for other areas of their life (Bill Clinton, for example. Virtue, as well as cognitive functions related to intelligence, deteriorates as willpower is depleted. Enough said).

So our heroic rider can't hold the reins of the elephant indefinitely. Willpower takes energy, and energy is a scarce resource.[9] And we need this self-control when making decisions, having difficult conversations, concentrating on a new or difficult task, coping with fears or dealing with change. It's why most of our actions are automatic, ritualised, scripted. It takes less energy, but the result may not be what we wanted. The bigger the change needed, the more the behavioural changes needed affect our limited willpower.

The Heath brothers argue, pretty convincingly, that we're maybe not as resistant to change as we generally think; we're just exhausted exerting the necessary willpower to go along with it.[10]

It's not all the elephant's fault, however. An unmotivated elephant can derail a change initiative, but the elephant needs direction – and it gets that from the rider.

clarity

This is the Heaths' third surprise – it may just be clarity of direction that's required. To our brain, change is either huge or at least feels huge, so it needs to be channelled and directed. It needs a well-defined path to follow – a clearly articulated direction of travel so once the elephant is motivated it knows where to go. And the surrounding environment needs to help the process, not hinder it.

---

8   In the discussion relating to emotional intelligence.

9   The Heaths cite an interesting study where people were assigned to one of two groups – a radish-eating group and a chocolate cookie-eating group, when both these foods were available and in plain sight. All participants were able to exert willpower when asked to resist the food. However, when asked to do a second, seemingly unrelated test, the radish-eaters were less persistent in solving puzzles. Their willpower had been depleted by resisting the cookies, whereas the cookie-eaters had a fresh rider. Full of chocolate. And willpower is inextricably tied to glucose.

10 Note to self; ask delegates not to think of a pink penguin for the duration of a training course. They'll be so exhausted that they'll be like putty in my hands. *Bond villain laugh*.

These three surprises, then, have three solutions: to change behaviour, you have to direct the rider, motivate the elephant and shape the path. In short:

- **Direct the rider.** Provide clear direction (for yourself and, if you're in charge of a change project, for your team). We return to some of these ideas in Section 5, but know where you want to get to. Start with the end in mind. It helps to focus on what's already gone well, what is possible, what skills and strengths exist, what works and how we can do more of it. This is very much in tune with the whole Positive Psychology paradigm we talked about in Chapter 9: focusing on the positive and possible is motivating in itself, and creates more of the same. Remember that we're wired to focus on the negative, to 'solve the problem' and to wallow in misfortune.[11] Focus on the solutions and build on what's already going well, and then script the critical moves to provide the direction. What behaviours do we need to make it successful? What specifically should we do? Why do we need to do it? What's the rationale? Work out the beginning, know what the ending should look like and the middle will take care of itself. Clarity is the enemy of resistance.

- **Motivate the elephant.** You can't control an elephant, just encourage it to go in the direction you want. Remember that emotion trumps logic and so we need to tap into our own (and others') feelings. According to John Kotter, who we met in Section 1, our implicit model of change is ANALYSE–THINK–CHANGE, and this is often what our workplaces encourage us to do. No-one was ever persuaded by a spreadsheet.[12]

  To motivate the elephant, it needs to be more SEE–FEEL–CHANGE. We often speak to the rider to convince them, but we should be speaking to the elephant. To some extent, we need to generate emotion by creating a crisis – what Kotter calls creating the case for urgency (or noticing the burning platform). This may help get the critical motivation levels up, but for sustained change we need to tap into the more positive emotions, which broaden and build our catalogue of thoughts, feelings and behaviours. Negative emotions narrow our thought-action repertoire by preparing for fight/flight/freeze, whereas positive emotions create more options to use our physical, intellectual and social resources.

  Build your strengths, as we see in Chapter 14. And the more you can reduce the perceived impact of the change by reducing its scale into smaller,

---

11 This explains Morrissey.

12 OK, maybe some accountants.

more manageable nudges, the less agitated the elephant will get. It's more motivating to achieve small successes along a longer journey than to be at the start of a shorter one.

- **Shape the path**. The environment around us needs to be able to support and reinforce the change. We have an inbuilt tendency to attribute people's behaviour to them, rather than their situation – and often judge ourselves less harshly than we judge others.[13] The point is, make it easier to go along with. Create a downhill slope. If you're trying to lose weight, eating off a smaller plate makes you reduce portion size. Hide the marshmallow.

Some people, when they really need to concentrate, take themselves to a place with no Wi-fi to reduce the temptation to distract themselves with internet clips of cats falling off work surfaces. We also need to build the new habits – set arbitrary deadlines and goals (think SMART[14]) that can concentrate the mind. The Heaths call these action triggers – they prompt and pre-empt the next action so it builds and becomes a new habit.

Make a checklist and revel in the lovely dopamine hit when you tick something off. Finally, remember that elephants are herd animals and are influenced by the behaviour of others.[15] We'll be aided in our quest if we see other people performing these habits too, so notice what others do and enlist support. Behaviour, like the emotions that create it, is contagious.

As you're aware, these three vertebrate-based ways of thinking are all effectively saying the same thing. There's a tension between head and heart, logic and emotion – and when that tension exists, heart/chimp/elephant wins. To manage this process and then instil new habits for the human/rider is the way to go. We expand on how to instil new habits in Chapter 14.

---

13   Psychologists call this fundamental attribution error. This is why they never get asked to name anything else.

14   Goals that are Specific, Measurable, Achievable, Relevant and Time-bound.

15   I explored group psychology and its implications in *The Psychological Manager: Improve Your Performance Conversations*.

14

strengths and positive habits

So. We've taken charge of what we can take charge of and let go of the rest. We've mastered our mindset by reframing. We're acting more like scientists by challenging those unhelpful beliefs that lead, inexorably – through attitudes, thoughts and feelings – to our behaviour and the inevitable result. We've chosen our attitude, temporarily put our chimps in the box and directed our elephant's rider. Let's shape the path a little more by capitalising on our strengths and instilling more effective habits.

In Chapter 9, we invited you to identify your key work-based strengths using the Strengthscope© model. These are the key ways in which you're energised at work – by ensuring that you're able to demonstrate them. You on a good day. We also suggested you answered the questions in Appendix 12, which ended with 'How can I do more of it?' Let's expand on how we do this.

forming positive habits

Think back to the principle of confirmation bias. Remember that we tend to cherry-pick the evidence available to support our existing beliefs and rationalise any that contradict them. Everything is an interpretation and it's uncomfortable to challenge what we already believe, so we don't.

This works for habits, too. We tend to go along with our habitual ways of behaving because it's cognitively easy (the script is already written and learned) and it's stressful for us to challenge them. The implication of this is that unhelpful or negative thoughts and behaviours promote another set of unhelpful or negative behaviours. Likewise, positive, helpful thoughts and behaviours promote more of the same.

In a way, this whole section has been leading up to this. One of the best ways to increase our resilience is to focus on the positive instead of our automatic default of focusing on the negative.[1] This goes against the grain somewhat, but it's the difference between a spiral into learned helplessness or into learned optimism. And we do it through promoting and reinforcing positive habits. As long as it's grounded in some sort of reality, there's an argument for saying that as a mindset, optimism is healthier – even physically – than pessimism. Optimists deal with failure constructively by treating it as a learning exercise.

broaden and build

When we focus on more positive thoughts, feelings and behaviours, we increase our repertoire of actions. Psychologists call this the Broaden and Build concept.[2] Positive emotions (such as interest) promote positive behaviours (such as exploring opportunities). This leads to an increase in our options for behavioural responses. Negative emotions (such as worry) tend to narrow our thought-action repertoire to encourage us to focus on life-saving activities such as avoiding mistakes (like accidentally putting a knife in the fork drawer). Essentially, negative mood states prepare us for fight or flight, and most of the time we don't need to do either. Focusing overly on the negative limits us and our achievements. And as we've seen, we have an in-built negativity bias as it is. Theorists such as Barbara Fredrickson suggest that Broaden and Build as a habit results in an increase in our intellectual, physical, social and psychological resources.

If you can train yourself to focus on positive feelings during times of stress, then you increase your ability to deal with it and identify (and ultimately create) more options to address the stressful situation. This isn't easy, because your brain wants to do exactly the opposite to avoid cutlery-related or other disasters.

---

1   Psychologists, with their usual flair, call this negativity bias. As already discussed, we have an inherent tendency to pay more attention to negative emotions, experiences and information than to positive ones. Bad is stronger than good.

2   Presumably to counter the Search and Destroy one.

By increasing our self-awareness, we know when these negative thoughts and feelings are occurring and can start to put measures in place to mitigate their effects – by taking charge and reframing. Even something as simple as saying 'Yet' when we tell ourselves we can't do something, becomes a productive habit.

Here are some classic (bad) thinking habits that we look at in Appendix 14:

Thinking habit	What it is	What you might say
Catastrophising	Assuming a worse-case scenario	This is awful; I'll never do this
Generalising	Seeing things in absolutes	This always happens to me; everybody dislikes me
Judging	Passing emotionally charged judgements on yourself or others	I'm worthless; they're hopeless and should've done better
Mind-reading	Making hasty assumptions	They thought I was dreadful; I know what they're thinking
Predicting the future	Foreseeing results	I know what will happen now; now they aren't going to trust me again

growth mindset

Our first step towards developing more positive habits to increase our resilience is to focus on growth – moving towards, not away from what's possible, or what can't be done. What you can do eventually, not what you can't do now. If you believe that your success (and by extension, your resilience) is based on innate ability and there's little you can do about it, then you limit your choices. If you believe that your success is based on hard work, learning and self-development, then you're not bound by the prison of your failures; they simply become learning opportunities. It wasn't successful *that* time. I can't do this *yet*. If I do this, then I will.

Part of the answer here is about trying to connect with your future self.[3] Research has shown that the more emotionally connected you are to your future self, the more you'll incorporate it into your current thinking, lifestyle

---

3   No, you don't need a DeLorean.

and maybe even budget. Think pensions – an exercise in long-term delayed gratification. It's having the second marshmallow by waiting. This is beginning with the end in mind all over again. Think about what you want your future to look like and put yourself there. Try to connect emotionally with that version of you. What does future-you see, feel or hear if you can make positive choices for yourself now? If you're living that future now, how do *you* feel?

Let's return to growth mindsets. Carol Dweck found that students with a growth mindset rather than a fixed mindset demonstrated higher levels of resilience and academic buoyancy. They focused more on learning rather than pure performance; it's less about winning and losing and more about growing and developing. Failure becomes less stressful because we still learn from the experience and can frame it as such.

This mindset, although a belief and a habit, is ultimately a choice. Do you focus only on performance, or temper this with what you've learned? It's a question of balance. The trouble with having a fixed, performance-only mindset is that you can never win. There's always another hill to climb. And when we eventually fail, as we all do at some point, we feel helpless and hopeless. Having a balancing focus on growth and learning mitigates this. Look again at the challenging of assumptions made in Appendix 14. It may look like this:

Thinking habit	What you might say	Challenge
Catastrophising	This is awful; I'll never do this	• Is it really that awful? • I might not like it but I can cope and it'll soon be over • What evidence do I have for saying I'll never do this? • When have I done something similar? • Who can I learn from who does this well? • What positives can I take from the experience?

flow (again)

And remember in Chapter 9 when we talked about being in a state of flow? This is when we're fully absorbed with what we're doing, and usually means performing at our absolute best. In this state, we persist with challenging tasks and develop our skills. This usually happens when you apply, mindfully, your key strengths to the task in hand.

The trick to achieving a state of flow more often, therefore, is to look for ways in which you can use your strengths rather than it just happening. What opportunities are there around you, or can you create, for you to demonstrate your strengths?

Go back to your top seven strengths you identified in Appendix 11. Ask yourself the following questions for each strength (Appendix 15):

- What activities allow me to demonstrate this strength?
- What results typically flow from this?
- When have I used this strength to overcome challenges?
- How can I increase my knowledge and skills in this strength? Where?
- What extra activities can I undertake to demonstrate this strength to myself (and to others)?
- How can I build this into my regular routine?
- How can I ensure that I don't overdo this strength? How will I know?

There's growing empirical evidence that playing to and using your strengths leads to increased resilience and vitality, decreased stress levels and increases in self-esteem, confidence and happiness. What's not to like!

habits

We also need to turn these positive thoughts, actions and strengths-based behaviours into habits. Habits are things we do without thinking. When activities or behaviours are truly a habit, we don't need to actively motivate ourselves to do them. When an activity requires us to generate the will to do it, all of a sudden we find a myriad of excuses as to why cleaning out the fridge is of vital importance.[4] It takes energy, and energy is a scarce resource. It may help to break bigger changes into smaller, more manageable ones.

---

4   Not that this has ever happened while writing this book. Ever.

forming new habits

The first step is simple: decide what we want to be a new habit. This needs to be as specific and concrete as possible (think SMART objectives again – there's a template in Appendix 16) and you have to *want* it. This is true of any of our (or our team's, for that matter) work behaviours or performance on a task – *will* trumps *skill* every single time.

We then need to set up triggers to aid our memory. Eventually, these triggers will be your own memory, but as this takes a while (many writers suggest it takes six weeks to really integrate a new habit), to start with you may need external triggers such as rituals – the old knotted handkerchief trick. Some people use elastic bands on the wrist[5] and others use little alarm messages on their smartphone.

You may also think of friends who can act as memory prompts (you can act as habit-forming buddies). Research[6] has shown that if you can find a way to make the prompt visual (such as moving a pile of paper clips from one jar to another every time you behave in accordance with the habit you're trying to instil) then this makes the habit stick. This is why:

- Visual clues act as a prompt and reminder to perform the habit initially.
- They help you to display your progress.
- This eventually generates its own motivation.

The whole process relies, of course, on repetition. Instilling new habits is like learning a language – we need to lay down the cable by repeating the thought-behaviour link until our neurons get used to the pathway. Breaking larger behavioural changes into smaller manageable chunks helps. Celebrate the small successes, and build on those previous successes. This taps into how our brain likes to work – gentle nudges with a reward for achieving them.

Try as well to make it hard not to do it – actively set up barriers to make it really difficult not to do the new behaviour. Research suggests that goals are 33% more likely to be achieved if you simply write them down. And remember – this is hard, so go easy on yourself! You're changing your brain's connections while doing this. This is real-life neurogenesis in action. This is real 'shape the path' stuff.

---

5   Preferably your own.

6   See James Clear's free download, *Transform Your Habits*.

stress as challenge

The 'stress' of doing this is actually beneficial. In Chapter 9 we mentioned the inverted U of the stress curve[7] and that we need some stress to motivate ourselves until we get to the top of the curve – we can just choose to call it *drive*. If we reframe this stress as challenge or drive, we can learn (again, by instilling new habits) to view it as positive. The main chemical at play here is noradrenaline, and it's an important one. According to some psychologists[8] this is the one that integrates working memory, arousal, awareness and sustained attention. Noradrenaline pushes you to the sweet spot at the top of the stress curve – optimal performance and, arguably, resilience. Flow sits in the middle of boredom and stress. It helps us to focus – and a wandering mind makes us feel out of control and can have an impact on happiness.[9]

There's a road in Kuwait[10] that's very long, very straight and surrounded by featureless desert. This is potentially very dangerous. The brain doesn't like long stretches of featureless desert. It gets bored. It switches off. It's not the most helpful thing it can do when it's supposed to be helping the driver. The solution to reducing the inevitable accidents was to put burnt-out wrecks of the vehicles that didn't make it at regular intervals on the side of the road. Our brain needs challenge to sustain its attention – and it's noradrenaline that creates this feeling of challenge as a response to the external stimuli of a burnt-out vehicle. We need this stimuli of a complicated environment to help us grow our brains to deal with it.

So, gentle, goal-directed stretch is good for us. It helps our brains grow through a process of self-directed neuroplasticity and creates neurogenesis.[11] The trick is to stretch, but not too much. We don't want to tip over to the downward bit of the Yerkes-Dodson curve. That's 'real' stress. We need to break out of our comfort zone (old habits) and stretch ourselves to integrate new habits. Our brains have to somehow override the urge to activate the old habit and replace it with the new one. This literally reshapes the brain. It's hard and uncomfortable, but this is where the magic happens.

---

7   Yerkes-Dodson.

8   Professor Ian Robertson, to name just one.

9   Robertson quotes a study where participants were doing a boring household chore; when their minds wandered, they reported lowered mood states compared to those who focused (reported in *The Psychologist* (2016) Vol. 29, No. 11). When our minds wander they tend to wander in a negative direction, because the brain hates unresolved conflicts and so goes back to try to resolve them.

10 To be fair, there may be more than one. I haven't been.

11 I'm unduly excited by this sentence.

getting support

This whole process of developing positive habits becomes a lot easier if you enlist the support of those around you. Not only will this keep you on track, it will actually generate motivation by improving your self-confidence and providing reassurance.

Don't forget that we're essentially wired for social interaction and connectedness. Supportive relationships have long been known to help our self-image and wellbeing – from Bowlby (attachment theory) through Maslow (hierarchy of needs) to the Positive Psychology movement promoted by Seligman, among others. Emotions and positivity leak just as much as negativity and fear.

A great deal of our brain circuitry is rooted in our relationships with others: it only takes 33 milliseconds to respond to facial expressions, for example. This is before you know they're there. One theory is that we very quickly and unconsciously mirror another's facial expressions to 'try them on for size' – to see how it feels. We then generate the same feeling state that the other person is likely to be in, so hey-presto – empathy!

Interestingly, one experiment found that people who'd had facial botox injections couldn't read others' facial expressions very well because their own faces couldn't move freely. The result was that they couldn't feel the same emotions. Watching someone else in pain and being in pain ourselves activates the same circuitry. This enables us, of course, to enjoy films and novels – without empathic understanding, we miss the point and feel detached from the narrative.

four communication styles

Of course, this means you need to avoid the Mood Hoovers. We all know people who suck the joy out of life, whose extreme negativity and pessimism make us wonder why we got up that morning. When we feel at low ebb, or are just working on our resilience, we need to avoid the Eeyores of life.[12] We need to find supportive learning partners who'll respond to our efforts, ideally from the first of these four communication styles (after Gable et al (2004) – cited in *Positive Psychology* by Bridget Grenville-Cleave):

- **Active Constructive**: you get unbridled support, allowing you to celebrate the good things that've happened, even if it's just a small step along the way.

---

12 You know the type. They usually say things like 'Yes, but that would never work here' or 'Yes, but you haven't considered this' or 'Well, we'll all be dead soon anyway'.

These people give full, undistracted attention and you feel motivated to continue.

- **Passive Constructive**: you get understated and rather unenthusiastic responses. A simple 'Well done' doesn't really cut it here. Ask them to say it once more. With feeling.

- **Passive Destructive**: they tend to turn the conversation back on to them. 'Well, that's all well and good, but this is what happened to *me* ...' is typical, as is 'You think *YOU* have problems, listen to *this* ...' Energy is sucked from us to bolster them. Mood Hoovers. Avoid them if you need a boost. You won't find it here.

- **Active Destructive**: really avoid these people unless you have the strength to just laugh inwardly at them. Such people actively (but maybe unconsciously to make themselves feel better) belittle your efforts or put a negative spin on your successes. They suck the joy out of life like a Psychological Vampire.[13]

Obviously, it helps if we have strong, positive relationships around us in our family or personal life. It helps our mood and self-esteem and gives us more energy to focus on the positive. Happiness is contagious, so if you practise the Active Constructive style, you're more likely to get it back.

Not everyone has this luxury, however, so we need to apply these principles to our friends, acquaintances and work colleagues. Just choose them carefully. It may be that those closest to you aren't always the best people to help you on your resilience journey – sometimes, a couple of degrees of separation helps.

who can help?

The worksheets in Appendices 17 and 18 may help. Populate them with names, and at the same time think of specific ways that they can help you. It may be that some are there just because you can watch and learn; others, you may want to ask them specifically if they're prepared to help you. Many of us tend to wait until we need help before we ask for it. Be proactive. Get the ball rolling now. And, of course, you may be able to help them too, and share the journey.

and think about you

Remember that you're also half the equation. Think about how you typically respond to those around you. Do you easily trust people? What are the

---

13 You might hear 'Well, don't forget you're only half-way there' or 'You wait – it probably won't work'. Definitely Avoid, don't Marry and try not to Snog.

implications? What happens to your patience and interpersonal skills when you're under pressure? Are you a Mood Hoover to others?

If you are, or have a tendency to look on the less-bright side of life, then others may be less willing to help you (especially if they read this book and put you in the 'Who drains me of energy?' section of Appendix 17).

One final note. It may be, occasionally, that all of this isn't enough. There's nothing wrong with seeking professional help from a coach, counsellor or therapist should the need arise. It's not a sign of weakness – indeed, recognising that you need another level of support for a period of time could well be one of your more productive habits.

And above all, throughout all of this, be kind to yourself.

look after yourself

No book on increasing resilience is complete without a chapter that tells you not to drink gin and to get yourself a good night's sleep. This chapter isn't going to do that. Well, it is, but let's get a sense of perspective. Most of this falls into the realm of common sense. We all know this anyway, but it helps to have a reminder if you need to be especially kind to yourself at the moment. Frame it positively – these are ways to help your brain function effectively, so you're better placed to do all the reframing and limbic system management.

be kind to yourself

Eat the marshmallow occasionally, while shouting 'Take *that*, Walter Mischel!' They're very nice, and life is for living and enjoying marshmallows. But make it a conscious choice.

diet

It's a generally recognised fact that we're made of about 70% water, and our brains slightly more (78% according to some neurologists). When we're dehydrated, our mental functions rapidly deteriorate. Sipping limited water when lost in a desert may not help you survive any longer, but it will help to keep you sane and functioning. So, keep hydrated and be careful of caffeine intake, which can dehydrate you if you have too much[1] and can increase adrenaline levels and lead to higher blood pressure in some. If you have to spend some time concentrating, have a glass of water for optimal performance.

You may notice that when you're concentrating (on a training course, studying or really having to focus on the latest *Star Wars* movie) that you crave glucose/popcorn. We covered the energy-heavy aspect of the brain in Section 2, which is why we go down the path of habits, rituals and scripts to aid this search for efficient use of resources. So when we have to concentrate, eat little and often – as the brain is unable to store energy.

A diet rich in Omega-3 oils can help brain function[2] so eat nuts, seeds and oily fish. Studies have shown that Omega-3 can reduce impulsiveness and even pessimism. Fresh fruit and vegetables (especially the darker, leafier kind) have more antioxidants, which can help brain function – as can a nice cup of tea. Certain foods can help produce neurotransmitters, the chemicals that pass signals from one brain cell to another: for example, serotonin production is boosted by eating carbohydrates, endorphins can be created by spicy food and chocolate, and dopamine by eating apples, fish and chicken, as well as green vegetables.

Let's get a sense of proportion here too, however. If you feel down, your brain tells your body that this probably means you're lacking in energy, so makes you want high-energy, i.e. calorific, food. This also has the effect of triggering the pleasure centres in the brain. It's why no-one ever eats a comfort-radish.

The time of day you eat has an impact, too. Skipping breakfast puts your brain on the back-foot right from the get-go. This can affect mood state and attitude, and reduce our ability to deal with life's challenges.

---

1   *Guilty look to camera*.
2   By helping to lay down myelin sheaths on the axons of your neurons, if you're interested.

booze and fags

Oh, and limit alcohol and don't smoke.[3]

exercise

There are so many benefits to exercise and so many books on the subject that this isn't the place to extol its virtues (which are general health maintenance, circulation, weight management, heart and lung function). It's been shown that exercise can help moderate anxiety and depression. It even gives you more energy, which is the usual retort gym coaches use when people say they're too tired to exercise!

There you go. Consider yourself reminded.

However, many people are less aware of the effects exercise can have on the brain and our mood state, which makes it relevant for this book. Regular exercise can improve brain function within weeks[4] as blood flow and therefore increased oxygen helps keep blood vessels in the brain healthy. It also helps to dissipate those nasty stress chemicals that can interfere with learning and concentration – which is why a good walk,[5] game of squash or repeatedly punching a picture of your boss can help with the amygdala-hijack – and releases dopamine which can help decision-making. Exercise also appears to release a chemical into the brain called *brain-derived neurotropic factor*, which helps to grow neurons. It can release endorphins, which are the body's painkillers, and can even give a feeling of euphoria. Which is nice.

So. Walk more. Get off the bus or tube a stop earlier than normal. Walk upstairs rather than take the lift. Do stretches or yoga moves while watching television. Go running or swimming as a self-reinforcing habit.

sleep

Sleep has many functions, and one of them is to help the brain to repeat connections it made during the day (which sometimes appear disguised as

---

3   Obligatory Public Health statement.

4   John Medina, Director of Brain Centre for Applied Learning Research at Seattle Pacific University, is the expert on this.

5   Millar & Krizan (2016) suggest the increase in positive mood when walking (they call it *incidental perambulation*. Scientists, eh? Never knowingly under-jargoned) is connected to how we evolved to find food and water.

dreams) and consolidate the learning. During deep REM (Rapid Eye Movement) sleep the brain connects old memories to new ones and new ones become reinforced. It is, essentially, the time when the brain does its filing. There's no actual consensus on why we evolved to need sleep, we just do.[6] Some believe it helps clear out waste products such as left-over neurotransmitters. Seven or eight hours seems to be the general view of what most people need; in addition, there's a growing body of evidence that a 3pm nap can aid concentration, but I was never able to convince my boss of this. What's clear is that early morning levels of cortisol help our brain to get started and perform, and this is generated from a good night's sleep. It can prime you for the rest of the day, increases the brain's willingness to learn and can also boost your immune system. Some have argued that dawn simulator alarm clocks help this process to be as natural as possible and can help mood state throughout the day.

shut 'em down

Interesting research has been published recently that looked at the effects of using technology in the bedroom.[7] Tablets and smartphones emit blue light, which is the sort of light that occurs at dawn (dusk light is more red-shifted) and so tricks your brain (via the pineal gland) into thinking it's time to get up by telling it to produce less melatonin. Using devices late at night doesn't exactly prime your brain for sleep!

Instead, have a writing pad by your bed so you can jot down any niggling thoughts that prevent you from going to sleep or from getting back to sleep in the middle of the night. This sort of gives your brain permission to switch off because it knows you can address these thoughts in the morning. Again, like all these things, it takes time for this to become a habit.

smile, smile, smile

Smile more. Yes, smile. It increases and releases serotonin and endorphins, which help regulate mood state and make us feel good. It leaks, too, so other

---

6   If you'll forgive a little ornithological indulgence, one of my favourite avian facts is that swifts often don't land for 18 months between fledging and their first breeding season. To do this, they go very high up at night and sleep on the wing while travelling in a large circle, like a plane does in a Heathrow holding pattern. They achieve this by shutting down one half of their brain at a time, presumably to avoid being hit by the 6am Boeing arrival from Malaysia.

7   No, not that. Don't go there.

people get the benefit. Some coaches encourage their clients to show gratitude for little things to help bolster mood. If you feel a bit low or fragile, make a list of everything (or at least three things) you have to feel grateful for. It can help give you a level of perspective, and again releases the feel-good chemicals. Research has shown that practising gratefulness can lead to increases in general happiness. Psychologists refer to this as helping to improve our sense of *coherence* – our belief that life is manageable, meaningful and understandable.[8]

This long Section 4 concentrates on increasing your own resilience, building on the focus on your own self-awareness in Section 3. The final Section 5 looks at what extra things we need to do when taking a team through change – something that not only requires all our own resilience, but also requires us to help our individual team members deal with it too.

---

8   Although why they can't just say that is beyond me.

section 4 summary: increase your resilience

This section hopefully answers the 'so what do I do with all this knowledge about brains?' question. Once we're self-aware, once we know what makes us tick and what definitely doesn't – and what our foibles and irritations are – we can start to challenge them, and not let them either define us or affect us unduly. Obviously, some things need far more than a book to help, but for many of us, the true remedy for our perceived lack of resilience is firmly in our own hands.

We talked about how to take charge of a situation by identifying what to focus on – and what to let go. We talked about mindset mastery and all that this entails – our ultimate reframe, if you will. We also talked about turning

(UNEXAMINED BELIEFS) » THOUGHTS » FEELINGS » BEHAVIOUR » RESULT

into

RESULT » BEHAVIOUR » FEELINGS » THOUGHTS » (CHALLENGED BELIEFS)

by beginning with the end in mind and not being seduced by the chocolate cake of confirmation bias.

We also used three famous models to help us; fish!, chimps and elephants. All these metaphors bring something subtly different to the table but all are essentially saying the same thing. Control what you can control by choosing your attitude and managing your initial emotions, while starting to challenge the beliefs that got you to amygdala-hijack in the first place.

Finally, we encouraged you to look after yourself by considering lifestyle changes that may help: diet, exercise, sleep and the power of a good smile.

Oh, and eat the marshmallow occasionally.

key learning points

1. The first step to increasing our resilience is to recognise what we *can* control and what we can't.
2. We can always control ourselves: our attitudes, thoughts, feelings and behaviours – and ultimately, our beliefs.
3. Beginning with the end in mind is an example of applying mindset mastery to what we can control within a situation.
4. Feelings are fleeting and may last no more than 20 seconds or so. After that, we do it to ourselves – and can therefore learn to control our feelings to help us, for example through things like distractor tasks.
5. Reframing is the ultimate mindset mastery technique. We can change how we view a problem, as ultimately our original view was only one of many. We can train ourselves to get a sense of perspective, or to see the positive elements to the situation. There's often something positive if you look hard enough. Remember – there are no facts, only interpretations!
6. Confirmation bias is the big lie we all tell ourselves to make sense of our world. Once we form a view, it's very difficult to change our minds about it because we skew the evidence in our favour, and don't act like scientists.
7. Many books on change use animal metaphors to explain them, be they fish!, chimps or elephants. Different animals, same principles!
8. Our way through resilience during change is to form new, more positive habits in a state of flow. We then broaden and build our repertoire of behaviours, instead of limiting them.
9. SMART objectives add structure and self-motivation through this process. Build small goals and tackle difficult things first. And write them down!
10. Don't try to do this all by yourself. Ask for support from your trusted friends and colleagues who typically have an Active Constructive communication style. Avoid the Mood Hoovers. And look after your health.

exercises

1. Use the circle of control in Appendix 13 to put the various components of any problems or challenges in the right circle. Ensure that you focus your energy where you can control or influence the situation. Be sure to identify *how* you can do this.

2. Practise challenging bad habits and attitudes using the worksheet in Appendix 14.

3. Think about your confirmation biases and Gremlins. We all have them. How can you challenge them? Why should you? What evidence can you find for them? How can you turn your Gremlins into Autopilots?

4. Remind yourself regularly of your key strengths. Identify how you can turn up the dial on them to help you achieve flow – find your own Goldilocks zone, something that's just right – between boredom and stress.

5. Expand on your strengths repertoire by completing the worksheet in Appendix 15.

6. Find support. No-one has to do all this by themselves. Identify constructive learning partners and help each other.

7. Practise being in uncertain or novel situations, and recognise how you can cope with them just fine. And don't forget to celebrate those successes!

section 5

take your team through change

'When we are no longer able to change a situation, we are challenged to change ourselves'
Viktor Frankl

'If you can't change the people, change the people'
Every chief executive, ever

chapter 16

take your team through change

In many ways, we're back at the beginning. We started our journey looking at the notion that change is (usually) necessary because of the internal and external drivers that are a constant tap on the shoulder.[1] We then looked at the biology and neurology of change before turning our attention to the remedies for ourselves: self-awareness and then increasing our resilience. Our final section addresses the extra things we have to do if we're responsible for managing a team through this heady process.

it's no democracy

Here's a quote on how to bring about change. You may have a view on this, but there's at least an element of truth in it. See if you can guess who it is:

The change is proposed; it is denounced as a disaster; it proceeds with vast

---

1   A perfectly good riposte to 'We've always done it like this' is 'That's probably why it needs to change'. Stand at arm's length, though.

chipping away and opposition; it is unpopular; it comes about; within a short space of time, it is as if it had always been so.

This can work for some elements of government policy, for example. Think how vehemently people opposed the introduction of the compulsory wearing of seatbelts in cars; the banning of smoking in pubs, on the London Underground and in aircraft; charging for plastic bags; ~~the invasion of Iraq~~. Yes, that's right, the quote is from Tony Blair.

He sort of has a point. Many of us think that the imposition of the change is a diabolical liberty and will never work, and then we very quickly get used to it *and can't imagine it any other way.*

If there's one thing we can take from this, it's that management is not a democracy. If you're charged with taking a team through change, then often it's been imposed on you from those above you, and you have to implement it. It may also be a change that you yourself can see is necessary after being all leader-ly and doing a PESTLE analysis. A leader's job is to create the change and make it happen.

There are ways of doing it, however. One of my recurrent themes in this book is that people generally don't like change. So they will resist, or at least grumble a bit. Their chimps get agitated. The implications of Section 2 are quite profound. We're 'designed' through a process that gives evolutionary advantage to treat change as a threat – or even in some cases a bereavement. Which means that we tend to avoid it, or at least to resist it when it's imposed on us. And because our first reaction tends to be emotional, there's little point overselling the logic in the early stages of taking a team through change – *that* part of their brain won't be listening!

So, we have to do something in addition. The rest of this chapter looks at William Bridges' well-known model of change, which includes this additional bit and how it can act as a blueprint for your own change plan.

Bridges' Managing Transitions model

The first major insight that Bridges alludes to is simply that all the material we covered in Section 2 affects how people typically react to change, and therefore we have to do something with it. If we're going through change ourselves, there are things we can do to help ourselves, and if we're taking a team through change there are things we can do to make it more successful, by acknowledging our basic biology and putting things in place to mitigate its impact.

Bridges also distinguishes between a change and a transition: a change is the event itself ('We're all going to start hot-desking on 1 May'[2]) whereas it's the *transition* – the psychological readiness to behave in accordance with the change – that determines whether it will work or not. It isn't an optional extra – it's the transition that makes the change actually happen.

Bridges' model is deceptively simple. It's a three-stage process:

1. **Letting Go of the Old**. This first stage is the acknowledgement that things are ending, that there has to be a period of letting go psychologically – perhaps even to an existing identity – and ultimately deal with loss.
2. **Managing the Neutral Zone**. This is the in-between time, when the old is gone but the new hasn't yet arrived fully. This is when the crucial psychological adjustment takes place.
3. **Creating the New Beginning**. This is when we create our new identity, get used to the new way of doing things, and embed the new processes or thinking until it becomes the new normal.

The simple premise, therefore, is this: change of any sort succeeds or fails on the basis of whether those affected by the change start *behaving* differently. And this is determined by the way you deal with the ending of the old – a transition starts with an ending.

Letting Go of the Old

Before we can learn anything new, we usually have to unlearn the old way. It isn't changing to something new that people tend to resist – it's stopping what they used to do. Think back to Section 4; the first stage of learning a new habit is letting go of the old one. This is why overselling the positives of the new – no matter how logical or beneficial they may be to the team or even the individuals themselves – doesn't really work. We certainly have to give some of the rationale and the case for change, but we shouldn't go overboard with this.

Instead, we deal directly with the ending first. This isn't to say that we don't talk about the positives of the new – far from it – but the point is, this isn't what's going to make people change their behaviour. It's just not how we're wired.

Here's how we do it, according to Bridges:

· **Identify who is losing what**. In the planning stage, determine what exactly will change, who will be affected and in what way. What will be the (not

---

2   Now THIS gets chimps agitated. Think threats to status, territory ...

immediately obvious) knock-on effects? Ask yourself who is going to have to let go of something – physical things, status things, attitudes, comfort … Even if the change is already underway, it's not too late. Just ask people what they've had to give up or what they miss.

- **Accept the importance of the losses**. These losses are subjective but real to those going through them. Treat them seriously and with compassion. Remember that your view is irrelevant. You won't get commitment if you don't make the effort to understand.

- **Don't be surprised at overreaction**. It's their world that's changing and they may not feel they have a choice. Therefore, threat buttons are being pressed! You don't know what experiences people have had in the past or what previous small changes have led to in other parts of their lives. They may also assume – often from past experience – that the change is leading to something bigger. This doesn't mean that we avoid the change – far from it – but it does mean that we have to be prepared for big emotions that seem, on the face of it, out of proportion. Remember the bereavement cycle. Our brains don't distinguish well between levels of emotion.

- **Acknowledge the losses openly**. Bring them out into the open. Make it normal to talk about them. Admit that change may be painful for some people. We rarely make things worse by being honest about them. This doesn't mean we have to accept disruptive behaviour, and we may have to make it clear what's unacceptable, but we can at least acknowledge and understand the feelings driving the behaviour.

- **Try to help people find the 'what's in it for them'**. There may be things you can give back – after all, in your team's minds you may have taken things away, so this may help to achieve some sort of psychological balance. How can you give them more control, for example? What does it mean for future career choices, employability and skill development?

- **Communicate**. Then communicate more. Communicate the who, the what, the where, the when, the why and the how – as far as you know at this stage. Tell them what you don't know yet. Don't fall into the trap of telling yourself that you'll only upset people, or they don't need to know just yet, or assume they already know. They may know something and will start making it up anyway, so it's better to be honest about what you do know, what you don't and when you're likely to know.

- **Define what is changing (or over) and what is staying the same**. This can help reduce psychological tension and stress levels. After all, if absolutely everything is changing, then this is a complete restructure with all posts redundant and new posts to apply for. This is rarely the case. If we don't make explicit what needs to change and what doesn't, then people will make their own decisions on this which may not fit in with the strategic plan.

- **Mark the ending**. Have an activity or ceremony. Help to draw a line in the sand. Remember that our brains understand the world through story and narrative – so how can you help people picture the ending symbolically?

- **Treat the old ways with respect**. If you start acting as if the old ways were bad and you're going to save them from themselves, then this is a fast-track to limbic system overloads![3] Try to make any distinctions between the old way and the new way non-judgmentally. Helping your team decide what already works well that you need to keep can help here.

- **Finally, demonstrate how the endings they are having to go through ensures the continuity of what they care about**. This means their jobs, the department's success, reputation. An idealised past is just heuristics – cognitive biases or selective memory. They will already have made successful changes to get to this point. Remind them of this and how change can pave the way to future success.

Managing the Neutral Zone

Not dealing satisfactorily with Endings is a major reason why change-projects are often less successful – or at least, take longer to embed – than you'd like. Get this bit right and the rest becomes easier. The Neutral Zone, however, has its own challenges, not least the feeling of being trapped between a rock and a hard place. And remember that we're wired not to like ambiguity!

Just to add to the difficulty, you may find yourself under pressure from above, especially if you've spent some (worthwhile) time helping your team deal with the letting go. Forward motion seems to have slowed down, old certainties are less certain and the new ones haven't been built yet. This is often a period of anxiety, with reduced motivation and, ultimately, performance and productivity. Absenteeism may increase and teamwork undermined, as people retreat into looking after Number One.

However, it's not all bad. This is also a period of high energy and creativity. There may be more new ideas and the freedom to just try things out and see

---

3   Try to avoid the messianic approach. 'I am your Saviour, and everything you've been doing up until now has been rubbish' won't win followership and will merely lead to the digging in of heels. And before you know it, you've invaded a country again.

what happens. Chaos breeds life, order breeds habit! The role of the change manager is therefore to capitalise on this confusion by fostering innovation and creativity, while keeping the ship afloat and your team in one piece.

Here's how to do it:

- **Make this period of uncertainty feel normal**. Help people to understand that the journey takes time, that it's a process and that this stage is an important and necessary part of that process. It is not a wasted period of waiting, and it's important to give the message that it's normal to feel frustrated and 'on edge' during this phase. Perhaps you can find a team-appropriate metaphor to illustrate this period: a river of transition, or the winter before the spring, or even the last voyage of the old ship before it sinks! And remember – in uncertain times, people tend to follow those who demonstrate confidence that everything will be just fine.

- **Create temporary systems**. This gives some semblance of structure to this ambiguous time. You may be able to protect your team from other changes at this point or at least reframe them into 'It's all part of the bigger change'. Do new policies, reporting lines, roles and procedures need to be created, even if they're just temporary? Are there short-term and relatively easy goals that you can get your team to set? You may also need to manage expectations, within the team itself, with connected teams and with those above you.

- **Build strong relations with connected teams**. This may help reduce the feeling of being isolated or 'all at sea', and may help to stop old patterns or habits repeating themselves. Think about setting up communication channels or even newsletters to keep people abreast of progress, foster a feeling of 'We're all in this together' and starve the rumour-mill.

- **Depending on the size and scope of the change, you could consider creating a Change Team** (Bridges calls this a Transition Monitoring Team, Kotter calls it a Guiding Coalition). This team should be representative of the team at large and should meet regularly to discuss progress, troubleshoot and facilitate the solving of problems (but not doing it themselves), ensure that communication upwards and outwards is up to scratch, and report back to the group regularly. It also needs a very clear and explicit, not implicit, remit.

- **Finally, use this stage to really enhance the creative output of your team**. Capitalise on the breaks in the normal routine to encourage people to think differently. Use facilitation techniques (e.g. brainstorming, 6 Thinking Hats) to add rigour to this process. Model the process yourself to provide a steer that fresh, innovative thinking is not only OK but welcomed – and make sure there's no semblance of a blame culture. Creativity and innovation are the first casualties of a punitive, command-and-control-style culture. As much as you can, reframe mistakes, losses and setbacks as learning tools. Make sure you have some budget for training in new techniques and above all, encourage experimentation (with review systems in place).

Creating the New Beginning

If we successfully navigate our way through the first two stages, this last stage is where we reap the rewards. This is the release of energy into a new direction, where the 'stuff' happens and where there are physical signs that things have really moved on. Again, the Beginning is not necessarily the same as the official start date. Beginnings are when people do things differently. There's often a conflict of feelings here. The tension of the Neutral Zone has gone and its demise eagerly anticipated, but the New Beginning is also a scary time for many. So there's a curious mixture of relief and nervousness, of anticipation and resistance.

You will, of course, have outlined what the change is for. Your PESTLE analysis (see Section 1) will have determined the factors impacting on your team and worked out what the new direction of travel should be. It may have been given to you from above, but whatever the scenario, you'll have communicated the headline of the changes and their aims. If we do the first two stages properly, then people will be ready to hear the logic, rationale and purpose behind the changes in more detail. They may also be more willing to listen to the case for urgency (see the summary of Kotter's work in Section 1).

the Four Ps

Bridges identifies the Four Ps that we need to communicate here:

- The **Purpose** behind the change: what you're trying to achieve and why. Some of this will obviously have been communicated at the Endings stage but this is where we go into the detail. You may have to sell the problem before you sell the solution and, of course, you'll have done this at the Endings stage, but it certainly doesn't hurt to reiterate it now. What's the problem we're trying to solve? Why has this come about? How does this fit into organisational strategy? What will happen if we do nothing? If you, as manager of the team, are unclear about the answers to these questions, how can you find out? Successful New Beginnings are based on a clear purpose.

- A **Picture** of what the outcome will look and feel like. Help them imagine it. The Purpose is abstract – help your team to see it. What will people be doing? How will they interact with each other and with other teams? What will the office look like? How will work be organised? How will they feel? Use any visual techniques you can get hold of: floor plans, flow charts, organograms, maps. Can you arrange a visit to another team or even organisation that's successfully navigated something similar?
- A **Plan** for phasing the outcome. Help people know what they have to do and when. Some people will get all they need from the Picture, but many others will need more guidance and want to know what, when, where and how. They will need the plan of the *change*, and the plan of the *transition*. Remember, these are different. The transition plan is more people-oriented and starts with where the people are now; a change plan starts with the outcome and works backwards.
- Give each person a **Part** to play in both the plan and the outcome. This gives people new insight into problems and reduces the 'us and them' feeling. It taps into their existing knowledge and problem-solving abilities, and increases the feeling of ownership and accountability. Individuals will also feel an element of peer pressure and conformity – they won't want to let down their team members.

After you do all this, your role is to continually reinforce. You should:

- Be consistent in all your messages, make sure you behave like a role model by demonstrating the behaviours/following new procedures yourself and reward the new behaviours and punish (not punitively, obviously) any regression to the old.
- Try to build in quick wins and celebrate these successes. Change takes a long time and it's easy for the energy to slacken off. Rewarding small but constant successes keeps up motivation and drive, and keeps people in touch with the ultimate plan. Change requires focusing our – and others' – attention in the new direction for long enough for it to rewire the brain and become a new habit.
- And finally, turn up the dial on your performance management and team-building skills. You may find the checklists at Appendices 19 and 20 useful.

Bridges' model of change helps us to deal with the messy, sometimes irrational way we typically react and provides a clear three-stage process for getting the most out of people during change. If you read Chapter 13 (Of fish!, chimps and elephants) then you'll recognise the journey we have to take.

Change is inevitable, and where there's change, there's transition. Bridges puts this succinctly:

CHANGE + HUMAN BEINGS = TRANSITION

chapter 17

identify and influence your stakeholders

Chapter 16 takes us through the stages of managing our team (and also ourselves) through the change process. Without our team's buy-in, we don't get a successful *transition* into the new way of things. Although it makes sense to start here, it may not be just our teams we have to involve to make the change successful.

map your stakeholders

There are two main stages to stakeholder mapping. The first is to know who they are, and the second is to decide what to do with them.[1]

stage 1: who are they?

Appendix 21 can help you determine who your stakeholders are. We can define a stakeholder for our purposes as anyone who's affected by, or can affect, our change. It helps to spend some time on this to ensure you don't

---

1   So, like your friends and very probably your enemies.

miss anyone out. Brainstorm as long a list as you can – you can always reduce it later. It may help to define your particular boxes (we use the following, but make up your own or add ones if necessary):

- Those people more senior than you.
- Those more junior than you (your team).
- Peers (colleagues at your level in other departments).
- External relationships (suppliers, central functions, customers, students, unions).

It helps to think as widely as you can here. You may not realise initially the impact your change may have elsewhere, so follow the process through in your head. Talk to your team about it: do it as a group exercise as a way to get involvement and buy-in from your team.

The following questions may help:

- Who will be directly affected?
- Who will be indirectly affected?
- Who wants us to fail?
- Who wants us to succeed?
- Who else needs to know?
- Whose permission do we need?

So, the end product of this stage is your own version of Appendix 21.

The next stage helps you determine how much energy to expend with each stakeholder.

stage 2: Power vs Influence

Once we identify our stakeholders, we can map them on to a blank version of Appendix 22. This is a typical four-box grid where we pitch the amount of *Power* these individuals have over our change and the level of *Interest* they have in it.

Populate your blank version with the names you identified in Stage 1, based on your assessment of their levels of Power and Interest in your change. This helps you to determine strategically how much effort to expend with the various people you believe have at least some stake in what you're trying to achieve. There's not much point spending the same effort with someone who has little Interest in and no Power over your change as with someone who has a lot of Power, for example.

Let's look at what we do with each category.

- **Low Interest, Low Power**: People in this group need to be monitored, kept informed where necessary and not forgotten about; however, they're not our priority. Make sure the communication channels are open and involve them if you can to get them more interested – you never know when they may move into a role with more power!
- **High Interest, Low Power**: Again, keep them informed to try to keep their interest high as they may move into a position with more influence (or be able to influence those who do). You never know what their networks are like!
- **Low Interest, High Power**: We need to spend some time with these people. Maintain good communication, though tailored to what they need, and try to engage their interest using all your influencing skills. Make sure you keep them happy (it may be prudent to ask them what they need to know and how involved they want to be). But these are important people, so we need to get their interest levels up. What benefits can you sell relating to your change? How might it impact on them in positive ways? How does your change help them? Try to engineer regular touch-points to keep them up to date.
- **High Interest, High Power**: These are your key stakeholders. It's all too tempting to spend time and effort with only these, but as we've seen, that's missing a trick. Nevertheless, you need to manage them closely, communicate often and actively engage them in activities related to your change – if you can. Are there any specific high-level activities you can ask them to be involved with? Can they act as coach or mentor to members of your team? Can you tap into their networks? Can you ask them for advice? If you were in their position, what would you want? If you treat them right, they can be your key advocates.

Stakeholder mapping is a simple enough activity, but a little time spent thinking about these stages may save a lot of time later on, and will ensure that you don't forget to communicate or involve those individuals who can really make a difference to your change-project. The questions in Appendix 23 will help you focus your mind further on getting the best out of stakeholder management.

18

increase your influence and deal with resistance

One of the recurring themes throughout this book is that elements of our behaviour are hangovers from the past, and reflect our biology and neurology. When we first decided to come down from the trees, for example, and gradually colonised the planet (at the time of writing, about 78,000 years ago according to estimates[1]) we learned that we survived better in groups. Those that did, survived, and so passed on this genetic trait. Those that didn't had a rather lonely life, probably didn't get a mate and therefore didn't pass on anything.

the importance of rapport

We also learned that it was useful to be wary of those not in our group, troop or tribe, and therefore the stress response created by chemicals such as cortisol (who we met in Section 2) put us on our guard, ready to do the fight/flight thing. It really doesn't help you to bond with your own tribe if you do this all the time[2]

---

1   By the time you read this, you may need to add 18 months or so.

2   And this certainly won't get you a mate.

so a chemical (oxytocin) overrides the others – the group-bonding 'You're in my tribe' chemical. This therefore reduces defensiveness, makes us more open to experience and makes us feel like we belong.

This, essentially, is the main chemical behind rapport. And rapport is important, not just because it feels nice, but because we only buy from people who we feel are in our tribe, which is why salespeople spend a lot of money training staff to create instant rapport. Of course, buying doesn't have to be a product. It can also be an idea, a concept, or your change plan.

Here's our first principle of influence, then. Use this knowledge of the chemical basis behind behaviour. Pay into the emotional bank account and create rapport by building relationships before you need them. Do favours. Have a positive attitude. Try to keep the chimps of the people around you happy by belonging to the troop. We need to be engaging to get engagement. If people feel that you value them and their potential contribution, they're more likely to be influenced by you and help you implement your change plan.

You may be able to invite them to co-create the future you're trying to instil. Get them involved and give them ownership. Discuss with them what the future could look like, what's in it for them and the organisation, what *great* will feel like – and then what the steps are to get there and what you'll appreciate their help with specifically.

The more you can make this a conscious habit, the more it will stick. Your leadership, and your influence, is intrinsically linked to the quality of the relationships you build. We care what other people think of us and we go to some lengths to help people to like us; we can use this desire for 'impression management' to help move forward the change we're trying to instil.

It sounds obvious, doesn't it? But here's another little foible of the brain. The more we spend time focusing on *stuff*, on analytical thinking and problem-solving, our ability to empathise with others reduces, because these two networks are inversely correlated. The more you use one, the more there's a reduction in the other. It's a question of balance.

Let's distinguish between three related but different concepts:

- **Influence** is to change attitudes and/or behaviours of others without using coercion or deception. People (and teams) change, but you have influenced them. A real transition!
- **Persuasion** is similar, but with the dial turned up. We may have more of an agenda to push or more of a stake in the outcome. Most change will also require some of this.

- **Negotiation**. This is more of a process, by which we search for terms to obtain what we want from someone who wants something from us, in a way that means both parties end up happy.

It's influence (with an element of persuasion) that we're concerned with here, in getting our teams or stakeholders to behave differently.

Cialdini's 6 Laws of Persuasion

Robert Cialdini has written perhaps the seminal work on the psychology of influence; he came up with the 6 Laws of Persuasion, which he termed the *weapons of influence*. The basic premise of these laws is that we operate in the world using shortcuts to reduce the amount of data we have to deal with. We've met this concept many times before throughout this book – it's at the heart of our typical change responses and the need to mentally reframe to increase our resilience.

So Cialdini's 6 Laws of Persuasion are:

1. **Reciprocity**. This is the idea that we're motivated to return favours; we don't like to be beholden to others as it creates an uncomfortable feeling of tension (dissonance). This is why charities give a free pen with a marketing letter. We're motivated to repay the favour to reduce the tension. Often, the favour returned is worth more than the original act. A related concept is the Door in the Face technique (not literally). If you ask for a really big favour that's declined, people are then more likely to agree to a smaller request (maybe the one you really wanted all along ...).

2. **Consistency**. This is our often obsessive desire to appear to be consistent in our actions as we tend to see consistency as a strength – inconsistency is typically perceived as a weakness. Therefore, if we do someone a favour, we're more likely to perform another (often bigger) favour later. Again, this reduces the dissonance as we're motivated to behave in a way that justifies or at least is consistent with our earlier behaviour. Salespeople call this the Foot in the Door technique, and it often works provided there's at least some delay between requests – and the delay can even be weeks![3] It also works best when the requests are 'prosocial' – i.e. are perceived to be helpful or good. Most people are decent!

---

3   Studies have shown that the request can even be made online and still have a potent effect. Persuasion doesn't always need the body language, rapport and interpersonal niceties, it seems.

3. **Social proof.** This is related to the research into conformity, in that we often behave in ways that we see other people behaving. The shortcut here is that if other people are doing it, then it's probably OK and I should be doing it too.[4] Let's go back to being hunter/gatherers for a moment. Hunting in packs requires greater intellect, and it also requires greater division of labour and logistics. This in turn meant that we had to care about those who were outside our immediate family group (see the discussion on rapport above). The result is that in order to bond with this extended group, we may override our judgement to conform to group decisions, or even worse, Groupthink. A large part of our own identity is bound up in these relationships, and so we conform to fit in.

4. **Authority.** There's a wealth of research that suggests that many of us have a deep-rooted sense of duty to authority. This research supports the idea that we may do extreme things when instructed to do so by an authority figure – which, of course, may include high-profile or even celebrity endorsements for products.

5. **Likeability.** Essentially, we're influenced by those we know and like, and we tend to know and like those who are similar to us. This is the oxytocin effect described earlier. We're also influenced by those who are associated in some way with success and positivity – again, think celebrity endorsements.

6. **Scarcity.** Opportunities seem more valuable to us when their availability is limited. We're often motivated more from a fear of missing out than by a delight of gaining something – the well-known *loss aversion* cognitive bias. This is used in many 'last chance to buy' campaigns.

We can use these 'weapons of influence' to help us influence our stakeholders or our teams. Obviously, not all will apply to every change, but try using Appendix 24 to see if any of the principles can help you with your own stakeholder-influencing strategy.

dealing with resistance

Finally, what if – after all our efforts – certain individuals still seem to resist the changes we're trying to implement?

One useful model of understanding why people (our teams and even our

---

4   The research and principles of conformity and peer pressure (and also obedience to authority and Groupthink) are discussed in *The Psychological Manager: Improve Your Performance Conversations.*

stakeholders) may be resistant to our change is to ask these three questions (see Appendix 25):

1. **Is there a lack of awareness about what the change is about?** Your team or stakeholders may not be as aware as you are of the bigger picture – the reasons behind the change or the drivers for its implementation.[5] What will happen if nothing changes? How may the change affect the individual's job or working practices? How should they behave in the new way? What will change and what won't? In other words, why is the change happening and what does it actually mean for the individuals concerned? Remember *Switch* from Section 4: clarity dissolves resistance.

2. **Is there an unwillingness to go along with the changes?** Individuals may be aware of the changes but they either don't agree with them or just don't want to behave differently. How can you use the 6 Laws of Persuasion? Can you encourage small behavioural changes to start with? How can you tap into what really motivates them to get them to go along with the changes? Can you tweak the environment so that change is inevitable anyway? How clear are the consequences for non-compliance? What *are* the consequences for non-compliance in your organisation?[6]

3. **Is there a fear about not being capable of working in the new way – or a fear of the unknown or not being able to cope?** Is there a lack of confidence in skillsets or are there deeply ingrained behaviours that people don't think they can change? How can you encourage small steps and reward successes? How can you help identify existing skills and strengths that may just have to be applied in a slightly new way? What isn't actually changing at all? How can you shrink the change into manageable chunks to reduce stress levels? What training, coaching and mentoring can you provide?

Obviously, the only way to find out what's causing the resistance is to ask. Calmly, kindly, supportively. Use your coaching skills. See what small steps you can encourage. But above all, give them a good listening-to.

---

5   Think Nietzsche: He who understands the *why* can put up with almost any *how* ...

6   I'm long enough in the tooth to know that in some organisations non-compliance is a fast-track to a P45; in others, people are left to go stagnant; in others, they and their behaviour are just ignored and everyone hopes their toxicity won't leak. Note: toxicity leaks. Every time. We need to help people to understand that change is necessary and why it's necessary. There's a great quote by Julian Cope in *Repossessed*: 'The rejection of technology [for example] is only sound when it's done through understanding. Rejection through ignorance or belief in the natural superiority of the old ways seems to me to be as bad as drably accepting all modernism.'

Knowing who your major stakeholders are and how much time to spend with them is an essential part of your change plan. Only then can you identify who you need to influence (and maybe even persuade) and what your strategies should be. Remember that when a change project fails, it's usually because people don't behave in the ways necessary to support it.

Dealing with resistance to change is a balance of carrot and stick (not literally!) and it may be that you have to make clear the consequences of not changing – as a team and for the individuals concerned. However, most people are usually willing to make the change a successful transition if you follow the steps in this section.

And the thing is, it probably has to happen regardless. It just *is*.

section 5 summary:
take your team through change

In this final section, we turned our attention to other people; managing them through change – or perhaps more accurately, transition – and increasing our influence to make our change stick. Although Kotter (Section 1) talked about big organisational change, Bridges is more concerned with change on a smaller scale, and change that's more *people* oriented. Because it's people that make the change happen. To do this, we need to spend time dealing with the endings of the old because, as we've seen throughout this book, this is how our brains work – and it just *is*.

Of course, it helps us to know who'll be affected by our changes and where to spend the greatest part of our energy to make the change successful. We can borrow from essential project management techniques here to map stakeholders and to determine where the most value can be added in terms of our time and resources.

Finally, we looked at why people may be resistant to change and how we can help them.

Because it's probably going to happen anyway.

key learning points

1. We typically treat change as a threat, as we've seen throughout this book. Any model of change, therefore, needs to address this and acknowledge the way we're wired.
2. William Bridges' model of Managing Transitions does this by distinguishing between *change* (the event) and *transition* (the psychological buy-in).
3. To achieve this, we need to go through a three-stage process: Letting Go of the Old, Managing the Neutral Zone and then Creating the New Beginning.
4. These stages build on each other and need time to embed.
5. The new way, post-change, needs to be continually reinforced, rewarded and role-modelled by you.
6. Turn up the dial on your performance management and team-building skills.
7. It's vital to know who your stakeholders are and how much power and interest they have in your change.
8. There are two main stages to stakeholder mapping: categorising them and mapping them into Interest vs Power.
9. There are 6 Laws of Persuasion we can use to get our stakeholders on board.
10. Resistance may be due to one or more of three causes. It's useful to diagnose any resistance using this model.

exercises

1. Go back to Section 1 to remind yourself of *your* drivers for change.
2. Use the checklist in Appendix 20 to map your change on to Bridges' model.
3. Map your stakeholders using Appendices 21, 22 and 23.
4. Diagnose any resistance you find using Appendix 25.
5. Believe it will (and has to) happen, and don't forget to celebrate successes along the way!
6. Finally, buy 100 copies of this book and give them to your colleagues.

appendices

PESTLE analysis

	How could this affect my organisation or team?
Political	
Economic	
Social	
Technical	
Legal	
Environmental	

appendix 2
SWOT analysis

Strengths	Weaknesses
Opportunities	Threats

appendix 3
feedback-generating questions

1.	What do you think I do particularly well?
2.	What strengths do I demonstrate regularly?
3.	What can I improve?
4.	What can I be doing differently?
5.	What should I start doing?
6.	What should I continue to do?
7.	What should I stop doing?
8.	Do you have any other useful feedback for me?

appraisal-reflection questions

1.	What strengths have emerged over the years?
2.	How (and in what) have I grown?
3.	What have I particularly enjoyed over the years?
4.	When was I at my best?
5.	What developmental themes keep occurring?
6.	What have I done about them?
7.	What challenges have I overcome?
8.	What qualities did I use to overcome them?
9.	What do I want next year's appraisal to say?
10.	What can I start doing now to make this more likely?

appendix 5
self-reflection questions

Think about a time when you were under stress or pressure, or about a stressful or challenging time you're facing right now. Ask yourself these questions:

1.	What's challenging or stressful about it?
2.	What impact does it have on me emotionally? How do I know?
3.	Why do I think this is?
4.	How does it make me feel? What emotion could I call it?
5.	What do I notice physically? When did this start?
6.	What impact does it have on my colleagues or family?

self-coaching using the GROW model

Goal
• What's the issue or challenge?
• What will success or a solution look like?
• What's the end goal from this session?
• What's the ultimate end goal for the issue or challenge?
• When do I want to achieve a solution by?
• How will I know I'm successful?
• How can I measure progress along the way?

Reality
• What's the current situation as I see it?
• What actions have I tried so far?
• What was the outcome? How do I know?
• What haven't I tried?
• What's stopped me from trying this?
• What will be the impact on me? Others? The situation?
• Who else can help me?

Options
• What can I do to solve the problem?
• What else? (ad infinitum ...)
• What would I do if I had no restrictions?
• How real are those restrictions? Can I find a way round them?
• What have I seen elsewhere?
• Who do I know who's good at this? What can I learn from them?
• What are the advantages and disadvantages of my options?

Wrap-up
• Which option(s) am I going to choose?
• Why?
• What's the first step?
• When am I going to start?
• How will this (or these) help meet my original goal?
• What might get in the way and how can I prevent this?
• What support will help me?

appendix 7
self-guided mindfulness

With practice, you can effectively perform mindfulness any place, anytime, anywhere. But to start off, take 10 minutes or so to do it in more of a structured way. Follow these simple steps:

1. Relax as much as you can. Close your eyes. Sit up straight on a cushion or chair with your feet on the ground and your hands lying loosely and comfortably in your lap.

2. Do a little muscle-relaxing exercise – tense each part of your body in turn, then relax it. Start with your feet and work upwards.

3. Take three deep breaths – in for five seconds, out for eight seconds.

4. Just get into a regular, relaxed breathing pattern and count 10 breaths.

5. Keep this up in cycles of 10, but focus your awareness on the sensation of the air passing through your nostrils. Keep your awareness on this sensation; if your mind wanders, just gently bring it back without judgement.

6. After 10 cycles of this, shift your attention to the rise and fall of your diaphragm. Just notice the movement and again, if your mind wanders, bring it gently back.

7. After 10 cycles of this, do another 10 cycles, shifting your awareness from your nose in one breath to your diaphragm the next.

8. Gently open your eyes and breathe as normal. Try to notice how you feel. Give it a label.

Start with this exercise, then move on to noticing thoughts and feelings; don't judge them or interpret them, just notice them and move on. Try to practise this every day.

key motivational drivers
from the Blue Edge Motivation Questionnaire (BEM-Q©)

Affiliation: a desire to work closely with other people, getting to know them and being at the centre of social events
Recognition: a desire for acknowledgement for their efforts and receiving positive feedback from others
Caring: a desire to nurture others in the work role and being seen as a 'shoulder to cry on' by others
Independence: a desire to work autonomously without the heavy involvement of superiors, valuing personal freedom
Development: a desire for ongoing personal and professional development through training, coaching and other learning opportunities
Responsibility: a desire to take positions of responsibility and influence over others, valuing the status associated with those more senior positions
Achievement: a desire to set and achieve stretching goals, being recognised for achieving them
Variety: a desire to do original, creative, interesting work, valuing work environments which encourage innovation
Material: a desire to make money and achieve a good remunerative package
Security: a desire to work in a secure and stable role and organisation; more likely than most to believe in the 'job for life' model
Environment: a desire to be happy and comfortable in the physical working environment

dimensions of the 16PF™

adapted from Lord, W. (1997) *Personality in Practice*

Factor	
A	*Warmth*: level of readiness to become warmly involved with others
B	*Reasoning*: logical reasoning ability
C	*Emotional Stability*: perception of current level of coping with the daily demands of life
E	*Dominance*: strength of tendency to attempt to exert influence over others
F	*Liveliness*: excitement seeking and spontaneity of expression
G	*Rule Consciousness*: degree to which societal standards of behaviour and externally imposed rules are valued and followed
H	*Social Boldness*: level of ease in social situations
I	*Sensitivity*: the extent to which subjective feelings about issues influence judgement
L	*Vigilance*: likelihood of questioning the motives behind what others say or do
M	*Abstractedness*: degree of balance between attending to concrete aspects of the external environment and attending to thought processes triggered as a result
N	*Privateness*: likelihood of keeping personal information private
O	*Apprehension*: level of self-criticism and apprehension
Q1	*Openness to Change*: openness to new ideas and experiences
Q2	*Self-reliance*: strength of tendency to want to be around people and involved in group activities
Q3	*Perfectionism*: importance attached to behaving in line with clearly defined personal standards and being organised
Q4	*Tension*: level of physical tension as expressed by irritability and impatience with others

MBTI© dimensions

Extraversion: get energy from doing things and being with people. Sometimes talkative and their thoughts are often verbalised in real time.	*Introversion*: get energy from internal world of thoughts, reflections and feelings. Prefer to think through, rather than talk through issues.
Sensing: prefer to attend to – and stay with – facts and pragmatic details. Observant and often with a good memory. Enjoy the present.	*Intuition*: prefer to attend to patterns and meaning, rather than the facts themselves. Enjoy anticipating the future. Can be theoretical.
Thinking: prefer to make decisions based on logic and rationality. Like cause and effect reasoning and consistency. Task focused.	*Feeling*: prefer to make decisions based on personal convictions and from an involved standpoint. People and process focused.
Judging: prefer a structured, ordered lifestyle. Like to be scheduled and organised, enjoying decision-making and the planning process.	*Perceiving*: prefer to keep options open and being flexible and adaptable. Spontaneous and energised by the last minute time pressure.

appendix 11

Strengthscope© Strengths model

Emotional Strengths	
Courage: you take on challenges and face risks by standing up for what you believe	
Emotional Control: you are aware of your emotional 'triggers' and how to control them	
Enthusiasm: you demonstrate passion and energy when communicating goals, beliefs, interests or ideas you feel strongly about	
Optimism: you remain positive and upbeat about the future and your ability to influence it	
Resilience: you deal effectively with setbacks and enjoy overcoming difficult challenges	
Self-confidence: you have a strong belief in yourself and your abilities to accomplish goals	

Relational Strengths	
Relationship Building: you build networks of contacts and act as a hub between people	
Compassion: you demonstrate a genuine concern for the wellbeing and welfare of others	
Collaboration: you work cooperatively with others to overcome conflict and build towards a common goal	
Empathy: you identify with other people's situations and can see things from their perspective	
Persuasiveness: you are able to win agreement and support for a position or desired outcome	
Leading: you take responsibility for influencing and motivating others to contribute to success	
Developing Others: you promote other people's learning and development to help them achieve their potential	

Thinking Strengths	
Creativity: you come up with new ideas and original solutions to move things forward	
Common Sense: you make pragmatic judgements based on practical thinking and previous experience	
Critical Thinking: you approach problems by breaking them down systematically and evaluating them objectively	
Strategic Mindedness: you focus on the future and take a strategic perspective on issues and challenges	
Detail Orientation: you pay attention to detail in order to produce high quality output, no matter what the pressures	

Execution Strengths	
Flexibility: you remain adaptable and flexible in the face of unfamiliar or changing situations	
Initiative: you take independent action to make things happen and achieve goals	
Results Focus: you maintain a strong sense of focus on results, driving tasks and projects to completion	
Decisiveness: you make quick, confident and clear decisions, even when faced with limited information	
Efficiency: you take a well-ordered and methodical approach to tasks to achieve planned outcomes	
Self-improvement: you draw on a wide range of people and resources in the pursuit of self-development and learning	

appendix 12
three standout strengths

My three standout strengths are:

1.
• When did I demonstrate this?
• How did it help me achieve a successful outcome?
• When and how has it helped me meet a difficult challenge?
• How can I do more of it?
2.
• When did I demonstrate this?
• How did it help me achieve a successful outcome?
• When and how has it helped me meet a difficult challenge?
• How can I do more of it?
3.
• When did I demonstrate this?
• How did it help me achieve a successful outcome?
• When and how has it helped me meet a difficult challenge?
• How can I do more of it?

circle of control

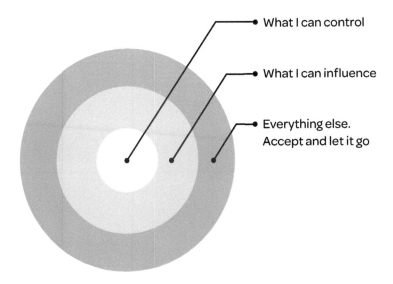

What I can control

What I can influence

Everything else.
Accept and let it go

appendix 14

choose your attitude

Thinking habit	What I might say	Challenge
Catastrophising	e.g. 'This mistake means that I'm going to lose my job'	e.g. 'Is that really likely to happen? What's my evidence for this? What's the worst that can happen? What good things have also happened?'
Generalising		
Judging		
Mind-reading		
Predicting the future		

build your strengths

For each strength, ask yourself these questions:
What activities allow me to demonstrate this strength?
What results typically flow from this?
When have I used this strength to overcome challenges?
How can I increase my knowledge and skills in this strength? Where?
What extra activities can I undertake to demonstrate this strength to myself (and to others)?
How can I build this into my regular routine?
How can I ensure that I don't overdo this strength? How will I know?

appendix 16
SMART objectives to form new habits

New habit: What do I want to achieve? Why? Is it a 'moving towards' goal or an 'avoidance' goal? Can I break it down into smaller sub-goals? How will I keep up my motivation? Who can help me?
Specific: What will I be doing when I achieve it? What might someone else observe?
Measurable: How will I know if I'm successful? How will I chart my progress?
Achievable: Is it too hard? Is it too easy? How can I ensure it's just right?
Relevant: How can I integrate this goal into the rest of my life?
Time-bound: What target have I set? What milestones along the way will help me monitor progress?

gain support

Who boosts my energy?	Who drains it?

appendix 18
identify learning partners

Who'll support me through my habit-forming? Who has an Active Constructive style?
Who could be a (constructively) critical friend? What can I request from them?
Who are my Resilience role models or mentors? What can I learn from them?
Who helps me keep a sense of perspective? When did it last happen?
Who can I be a role model for? Can I buddy-up with them as learning partners?

personal guidelines through change

Bridges, et al

Endings

- Keep a balanced perspective. What seems like an eternity to wait now will seem like a 'flash' in the years ahead.
- Confide in a trusted friend about the losses you feel and difficulties of 'letting go' of the way things used to be.
- Recall other endings in your life that unexpectedly led to new friendships, more gratifying jobs and wonderful opportunities.
- Take just 'one day at a time' and trust that everything you truly need, you'll have.
- Give yourself permission to feel your losses.
- Share your story with others.
- Stop fighting circumstances that are changing. Instead, accept their passing as an opportunity and reframe.
- Be willing to face what is happening. Test out the 'new realities' with a friend who knows you and can support you.

Transitions

- Look upon the time in between as necessary and valuable. A redefinition is taking place, and you are bringing completion to the past.
- Practise letting go of the old, so the new can emerge.
- Spend time learning about the change.
- Look for the opportunity. The 'what's in it for me?' is not always obvious. Keep looking.
- Stay in charge of your attitude. You can make your day as bright as you choose.
- Let go of the need to control.
- Feel your fears and do it anyway. Think of fear as energy in disguise.
- Reframe your perspective. Change negative thinking into positive. Practise optimism.
- Be open to new experiences.
- Seek and listen to all the career advice you can get. Move ahead on what feels right for you.
- Trust the process.

Beginnings

- Decide it is up to you to make the change work. Take personal ownership.
- Dive into the new situation with your full energy.
- Adopt new thinking, learn new tools.
- Take time to build relationships with the new team.
- See problems as the price of progress. Tackle them with high spirits.
- Make a decision to commit to the new goals and don't look back.
- See the positive change in your co-workers. This will help you see that you are changing too.
- Celebrate the small wins and early successes.

appendix 20
Bridges' Managing Transitions checklist

Letting Go of the Old	
Know who is going to lose what: what will change, who will be affected and in what way?	
Accept importance of losses to people. Be compassionate	
Don't be surprised at overreaction. To their brain, it's a threat	
Acknowledge losses openly. Bring them out into the open	
Help people find the 'what's in it for them'	
Communicate, then communicate some more – in different ways	
Define what is changing and what is staying the same	
Mark the ending in a team-appropriate way	
Treat the old way with respect	
Demonstrate the paradox of how letting go will help to keep what they care about	
Managing the Neutral Zone	
Make this period of uncertainty feel normal	
Create temporary systems to help create structure	
Build strong relations with connected teams	
Consider creating a Change Team	
Capitalise on, and enhance, the creativity and innovation this stage brings	
Creating the New Beginning	
Communicate the Purpose behind the change	
Create a Picture of what the future will look and feel like	
Create a change Plan for phasing the outcome	
Create a transition Plan to help the people get there	
Give each person a clearly defined Part to play	
Continually reinforce and role-model the change you wish to see	
Performance manage as usual – with the dial turned up	

map your stakeholders (1)

Map this for the people you need to influence

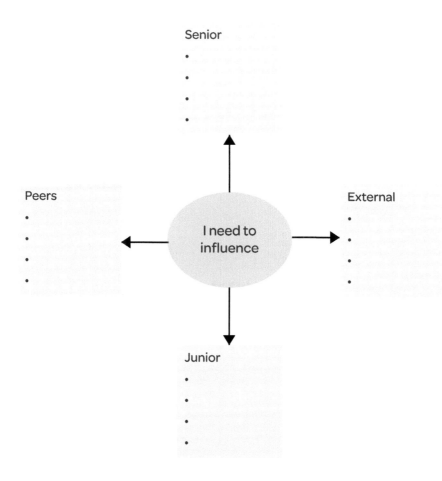

Senior
-
-
-
-

Peers
-
-
-
-

I need to influence

External
-
-
-
-

Junior
-
-
-
-

appendix 22
map your stakeholders (2)

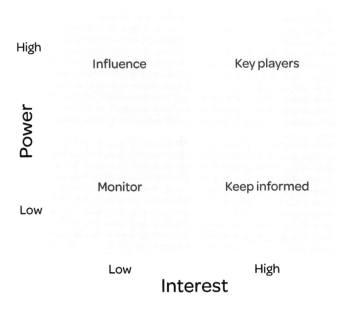

stakeholder questions

1. Who are my top five stakeholders? How can they each help me achieve success in my change project?

2. What are their key areas of interest or work objectives? What's really important to them?

3. What's my relationship like with each of these? How often do we meet, for example? Is this enough?

4. Which of my stakeholders has strengths where I don't? How specifically can they help me?

5. Are there any of my major stakeholders – and certainly those in my top five – who I don't have a good working relationship with? What is it that causes any difficulties/personality clashes? Different agendas? How can I take the initiative and do something about this?

appendix 24
Cialdini's 6 Laws of Persuasion

Think about how you can use the following 6 Laws of Persuasion to influence your stakeholders during your change implementation.

Law	What it means	Who can I use this with, to what ends, and how?
Reciprocity	We're motivated to repay the perceived debt owed to others	
Consistency	We're motivated to appear to act consistently with our earlier actions	
Social proof	We're motivated to do what others seem to be doing	
Authority	We have a deep-rooted sense of duty to senior or credible people	
Likeability	We're influenced by those whom we like and who are similar to us	
Scarcity	The fear of missing out is a great shaper of people's behaviour	

typical causes of resistance

Cause of resistance	Questions to ask
Lack of awareness	• Have I explained the reasons or drivers behind the change? • What will happen if we don't change? • What will happen to people's jobs or working practices? • What will stay the same? • What new behaviours need to be demonstrated? • How can I demonstrate them?
Lack of willingness	• Who do I need to influence and why? • How can I use the 6 Laws of Persuasion? • What small changes can get the ball rolling? • How will I celebrate these small successes? • What will motivate the individuals in my team? • Have I actually asked them what the problem is? • Have I made clear the consequences for non-compliance?
Lack of capability	• What's driving this – real or perceived lack of skills? • Is this just a lack of confidence? How can I help? • What's staying the same? • What existing skills and strengths do the individuals concerned have that they can use? • How can I encourage small steps and reward those steps? • What training, coaching and mentoring is needed?

afterword

If you make it this far, then by definition you've demonstrated your resilience, if not your dogged perseverance! I hope that you found the journey an interesting and useful one.

For some of you, this will be enough. For others, it may have whetted your appetite to learn more; if so, over the page there's a list of books that I find invaluable. Yet others may find this a prompt to get some professional help with areas of your life that you're currently struggling with. I wish you much luck with your continued learning. I also hope you find the worksheets in the appendices useful; you can download them at **www.thepsychologicalmanager.com**.

If you think I may be able to help you, your team or your organisation with training, development or coaching work, then please get in touch at the website above. I currently run the following courses in a variety of sectors:

- Becoming a new manager
- Managing performance and development
- Building your team

- Coaching skills for managers
- Managing change
- Increasing your resilience
- Influencing skills
- Understanding and using your strengths.

This book was two years in the making. My brain changed as a result of researching and writing it. Yours will have too, as a result of reading it. That's a good thing. After all, it's the only brain we've got. I really hope you think it was worth your investment of time and energy.

Thank you very much for reading it. And please – don't read horoscopes.

references and influences

To write this book I've drawn from the best my profession has to offer, other related and seemingly not-so-related works, as well as my own experiences as a manager, coach, facilitator and psychologist. The following books were – and still are – instrumental in my practice.

Adair, J. (2009). *Effective Teambuilding* (revised edition). London: Pan Books.

Bach, R. (1977). *Illusions; The Adventures of a Reluctant Messiah*. Arrow Books.

Bridges, W. (2003). *Managing Transitions*. London: Nicholas Brealey Publishing.

Brook, J. & Brewerton, P. (2016). *Optimize Your Strengths*. Wiley.

Burnett, D. (2016). *The Idiot Brain*. London: Faber & Faber.

Cialdini, R.B. (2007). *Influence: The Psychology of Persuasion*. HarperBusiness.

Covey, S.R. (2004). *The 7 Habits of Highly Effective People*. FranklinCovey.

Csikszentmihalyi, M. (1990). *Flow: The Psychology of Optimal Experience*. London: HarperCollins.

Dawkins, R. (1989). *The Selfish Gene* (2nd edition). New York: Oxford University Press.

Dawkins, R. (2006). *The God Delusion*. London: Black Swan.

Dweck, C. (2012). *Mindset*. Constable & Robinson Ltd.

Eagleman, D. (2016). *The Brain: the Story of You*. Canongate Books.

Eysenck, H.J. & Eysenck, S.B.G. (1964). *Manual of the Eysenck Personality Inventory*. London: ULP.

Goffee, R. & Jones, G. (2006). *Why Should Anyone Be Led By You?* Boston: Harvard Business School Press.

Goleman, D. (1998). *Working with Emotional Intelligence*. London: Bloomsbury.

Goleman, D., Boyatzis, R. & McKee, A. (2002). *The New Leaders*. London: Sphere.

Grenville-Cleave, B. (2012). *Positive Psychology*. Icon Books.

Heath, C. & D. (2010). *Switch*. Random House.

Herzberg, F. (2008). *One More Time: How Do You Motivate Employees?* Boston: Harvard Business Review Classics.

Kahneman, D. (2011). *Thinking, Fast and Slow*. London: Penguin Books.

Kotter, J. (1996). *Leading Change*. Boston: Harvard Business School Press.

Kotter, J. & Rathgeber, H. (2006). *Our Iceberg is Melting*. Macmillan.

Landsberg, M. (1999). *The Tao of Motivation*. London: Profile Books.

Landsberg, M. (2002). *The Tao of Coaching*. London: Profile Books.

Lord, W. (1997). *16PF5: Personality in Practice*. ASE, A Division of NFER-Nelson.

Lundin, S.C., Paul, H. & Christensen, J. (2000). *Fish!: A Remarkable Way to Boost Morale and Improve Results*. London: Hodder & Stoughton.

McCauley, C.D. & Moxley, R.S. (1996). 'Developmental 360: how feedback can make managers more effective', *Career Development International*, Vol. 1, No. 3, pp 15–19.

Mischel. W. (2014). *The Marshmallow Test*. Transworld Books.

Myers I., Briggs, K. et al (1998). *MBTI® Manual*. Palo Alto: Consulting Psychologists Press, Inc.

Peters, S. (2012). *The Chimp Paradox*. Ebury Publishing Ltd.

Radcliffe. S. (2008). *Future, Engage, Deliver*. Leicester: Matador.

Rock, D. (2009). *Your Brain at Work*. New York: HarperCollins.

Seligman, M. (1990). *Learned Optimism: How to Change Your Mind and Your Life*. Free Press.

Steers, R.M. & Porter, L.W. (1991). *Motivation and Work Behaviour*. McGraw-Hill, Inc.

Storr, P. (2012). *The Psychological Manager; Improve Your Performance Conversations*. Lulu Press.

Storr, W. (2013). *The Heretics: Adventures with the Enemies of Science*. Picador.

Webb, L. (2013). *Resilience*. Capstone Publishing Ltd.

Wellford, C. & Sykes, J. (2015). *Staying Sane in Business*. Sixth Sense Publishing.

Whitmore, J. (2009). *Coaching for Performance* (4th edition). London: Nicholas Brealey Publishing.

#0073 - 020517 - C0 - 210/148/11 - PB - DID1829714